the rookie
hockey mom

the rookie hockey mom

HOW TO PLAY THE GAME'S TOUGHEST POSITION

Melissa Walsh

THE LYONS PRESS
Guilford, Connecticut
An imprint of The Globe Pequot Press

The Lyons Press is an imprint of The Globe Pequot Press.

10 9 8 7 6 5 4 3 2 1

Printed in the United States of America

Designed by Maggie Peterson

Library of Congress Cataloging-in-Publication Data

Walsh, Melissa.
  The rookie hockey mom : how to play the game's toughest position / Melissa Walsh.
    p. cm.
  Includes bibliographical references and index.
  ISBN 1-59228-825-1 (trade paper)
  1. Hockey for children. I. Title.
  GV848.6.C45W37 2005
  796.962'083—dc22
                          2005015308

Contents

To Shane, Conor, Craig, and Marc—my stars.
Your twinkling brilliance warms and brightens each day.

Foreword

The ad read "Preschool Skating" and it sounded like a great idea to me. The moms could sit and visit with one another, while the little ones learned how to skate. After all, we lived in International Falls, Minnesota, right on the Canadian border. Surely my little boys should learn how to skate. That first day my oldest son, Jamie, was so excited I could barely get his skates on those wiggly little feet. He had spotted his friend Billy speeding around the rink and he couldn't wait to join him. Jamie literally ran out onto the ice and naturally he fell flat on his face. He looked up at me with tears in his big brown eyes and said, "I thought I'd be good at this." It was the beginning of my career as a hockey mom, and he had just given me my role. With no guidebook like this to follow, I unknowingly started with the last chapter of this book. I became encourager mom. Three more brothers would follow Jamie into sports, and I learned many other roles like schedule mom, driver mom, and what-can-I-eat-in-a-hurry mom. But being their number one fan was what I liked to be best.

Along the way hockey taught them a lot of life skills. The Pee-Wee coach stressed teamwork, the Bantam coach taught good sportsmanship, and the high school coach insisted on hard work. Still, at the end of the day the main thing always was that it should be fun. One son remembers moms with cowbells and silly hats at the state PeeWee tournament. Another remembers late-night talks after wins and later-night talks after losses. Yet another son remembers the mom section standing and singing "YMCA."

Over the years, our family took many mini vacations. In fact, basically we spent every weekend at an arena somewhere, eating concession-stand food and wearing a coat with a minimum of twenty different pins and buttons on it. It wasn't easy having four boys in different levels of their individual sports, but I wouldn't change that time for anything. Through the good times and bad, smiles and tears, new and lasting friendships were formed. Be the "cheerleader" for your child and enjoy every moment. Even now, though they are grown, they'll always be my little boys and there are still times when I need to be their cheerleader!

Patrice Langenbrunner,
mother of four sons, three who played youth hockey and beyond. NHLer Jamie Langenbrunner is her oldest son.

Preface

Imagine a single mom with no hockey experience trying to outfit a Pre-Mite. A few strangers in a pro shop offer her conflicting suggestions. Who is giving her the best advice? Ultimately she must develop her hockey-mom sense and figure it out for herself and her young player. And it's going to be tough since there is no definitive hockey-mom resource for her to consult.

Four years ago I was a neophyte hockey mom, a stranger at the rink. Just like the little novice skaters, I was fumbling and erring as I tried my darnedest to do it right. Since those days, I have learned a few things, a bit about whose advice has been good and whose has been poor. With countless rink hours still ahead of me, I thought I'd better dig in and really learn about this game. I discovered, as with most things, that it isn't until you start digging into a topic, that you have any notion of its enormity and complexity. Hockey is a grand topic and a grand sport—in scope, intensity, and its positive impact on a youth player's character and future.

True, most youth hockey players never get close to playing pro; rather they grow into adults who play recreational hockey or coach youth hockey. The love of hockey is a dynamic heritage that's passed generation to generation in my home state of Michigan and other northern U.S. states and Canadian provinces and is even being adopted in America's desert and tropical regions.

Those outside the hockey community might not understand the richness of the sport and its traditions. They buy into the sport's bad rep instead. Yet hockey does not teach kids to scream and fight. On the contrary, it molds them into young people with amazing self-control and a strong sense of discipline. They have an awareness of team and responsibility. You have to give the coaches and dads kudos for that, but don't forget to credit the moms. They are fundamental models of sacrifice and sportsmanship along the way. Though moms are so extremely important behind the scenes in youth hockey, I found, to my dismay, that there was no substantial one-stop, how-to resource for getting a new hockey mom started. Now there is.

We know that there are books to help mom with her other roles: caregiver, encourager, domestic diva, breadwinner, and homework helper to name a few. What about help with her role as her family's youth hockey manager? In the past, a mom's search for resources would lead her to coaching guides. *The Rookie Hockey Mom* now brings mom information that's more appropriate than Xs and Os, skills and drills; it is a one-stop guide to assist her in managing all of the non-Xs and Os of hockey, including:

- Hockey historical awareness
- Effective peace-at-the-rink strategy
- Hockey terms and lingo
- Hockey rules
- Officiating calls and signals
- Equipment purchasing and care
- League and program options
- Hockey schools and camps
- Injury prevention and care
- Team management
- Fund-raising
- Consoling and encouraging techniques

Most important, *The Rookie Hockey Mom* offers tips in what I call Heads-Up Hockey Parenting. Because I'm still a rookie hockey mom, I relied heavily on the advice and direction of veteran moms and former youth hockey players. I feel that they have collectively written this book through me. And during this project, they assisted me in tapping and developing my own hockey-mom sense.

I am grateful to many who have taken time to teach me about the overlooked and important business of being a hockey mom. My hockey-mom teachers include Barb Rittner, Lisa Keelan, Patrice Langenbrunner, Jeri Ruggeri, Anne Collias, Luanne Romano, Gracie Lucas, Jody Bruce, and countless others I've spoken with at my home ice of St. Clair Shores Civic Arena. Though I have never had the pleasure of meeting her, I'd like to also acknowledge the long hockey-mom career of Colleen Howe, whose amazing accomplishments and character I've read about with great admiration and respect. Mrs. Howe's hockey-mom career presents an enduring model of wisdom and strength to women both inside and outside the world of hockey. Thank you to Gordie Howe and Del Reddy for the photo of Mrs. Howe as a young hockey mom. Thank you to John Buccigross for permission to include his poem *Bless the Hockey Mom* and to hockey-mom columnist Pat Markham for allowing us to reprint a portion of her hockey-mom wisdom. Thank you to Craig Campbell and the Hockey Hall of Fame for sharing historical photos with us and for storing such an abundance of hockey historical information for the "history buff" hockey mom. Thanks also to Rob Rittner, Bill Rittner, Troy Barron, Matt Romaniski, George Collias, Tim Keelan, Darryl Moise, Shane Langenbrunner, and the folks at USA Hockey, specifically Dave Fischer and Harry Thompson, whose magazine and instructional materials are critical resources for any hockey parent. Thanks to Katie Reeves at the NCAA, who was such a great help to me. Thanks to Andrew Doig, Robert Cusmano, Paul Colombo, and George Bloomfield for Mini-Mite and Mite photos and to hockey-playing hockey mom Marie Cole. Thanks to photographer Bob Lash for capturing images of hockey moms playing hockey and allowing me to include two in this book.

I am grateful to the editors at The Lyons Press for their dexterity in editing my work while taking care to develop and enhance my vision for the book. Quality editing is an under-acknowledged art.

I must also acknowledge the great encouragement and support I received from my dear friend, Denys Vezinau, and my parents, Mike and Martha Walsh. My love of hockey is directly linked to the memory of my late grandfather Oscar Laperriere. As I wrote, my childhood memories at grandpa's were very vivid in my mind. These images of grandpa excitedly watching hockey games on CKLW-TV also warm me as I sit in cold rinks watching his great-grandsons play his beloved sport. He would be so proud.

Lastly, I extend a profound and tender thank-you to my sons for all that they teach me every day about heads-up parenting, and to God who handed me the amazing and profound charge of raising them for Him.

The Lesson of Puck Control

The hockey star is a genius at what he does.
—Colleen Howe, *My Three Hockey Players*

He shoots . . . He scores!" The words of Foster Hewitt echo in Mom's mind as she rises to cheer at a youth hockey game. She cheers for all the kids—though, quite naturally, it is her hockey kid who will forever be her heart's superstar.

Her child player isn't her star because of stats or raw talent. Her skater is a star because of how hard he works with his team to move the puck toward the net, maneuvering past and battling foes who try to knock him down. Her skater is a star because he is a "good" player. A good player carefully listens to the coach and respectfully heeds the authority of the referee. A good player gets up early for practice without complaining, practices drills on lake ice or in inline skates on the driveway. When faced with aggressive play, excessive or within the rules, Mom's skater continues thinking through his game, envisioning his team's next goal. The screaming from behind the boards is white noise. His focus is his game, honing instincts, and skills of feet, hands, heart, and mind.

And Mom's job has been a tough one—inconvenient, costly. She's had to endure obnoxious parents and cringe as her child gets bumped and hit. She can spot disappointment on her skater's face from the bleachers, through the cage hundreds of feet away, after a missed shot on net or a defensive tactic that was unsuccessful in preventing an opponent's goal.

She asks her skater after an extra tough competition or on the way to a 5 a.m. practice, "Are you having fun playing hockey?"

"Yeah," the player replies.

"Great," Mom says.

Mom signs the check for the next ice bill knowing first and foremost that her player's hockey development is owned by him, not by her. He defines his hockey dreams and craves the excitement of hockey's challenge. Mom is proud of her skater, because she understands that, by accepting this challenge, her child volunteered for a lesson that will support his development into an adult—the lesson of puck control.

Her skater will become an adult who will rise after getting knocked down. He will look to players of earlier generations to learn how to develop essential skills that enable him to carry a responsibility to net. He will jump over and maneuver around obstacles for his team, dedicated to self-discipline and self-control. Her skater will assertively and modestly dangle the puck up to its destination, and will do the same while serving in a job, heading a family, or volunteering for the nation or community.

As he grows, Mom's hockey player will start out each new morning with the words of Bob Johnson in mind—"It's a great day for hockey!"

1

History-Buff Mom

Hockey isn't much different than when I was playing. The rules haven't changed and the stars of today would have been stars when I was on the ice.

—Maurice "The Rocket" Richard, in
The Game I'll Never Forget, as told to George Vaas

I f you do not come from a hockey-loving family or have never played hockey yourself, you may have said to yourself, "So what's the big deal? They skate around after a puck, get knocked down a lot, go after the thing again, and infrequently score a goal." A superficial glance at the sport might lead to such a rudimentary perception of this dynamic sport. It's not until you dig into hockey's game dynamics and history that you can appreciate the sport as an endeavor well beyond its value of offering exercise. Ice hockey has much more to do with physical endurance and coordination, and it demands much more from its players than raw skill and strength. The sport contains facets of its own art, science, psychology, philosophy, and heritage. Learning ice hockey's history is a step in the right direction to gaining a proper sense of its strong appeal to players and fans.

Hilda Ranscombe (first row, first left), the acclaimed leader of the Preston Rivulettes, or "Rivs," was known for speed that rivaled boy players, even future NHLers. She is tributed in the Hockey Hall of Fame as an important leader in women's hockey. Her equipment is on display at Toronto's Hockey Hall of Fame. Photo credit: Hockey Hall of Fame

EVOLUTION OF THE SPORT

Ice hockey was not created in any particular snapshot of time. Rather it emerged gradually. Though its evolution has slowed significantly since it became an organized, professional activity, the sport's development has never been static. Ice hockey is a living thing, and youth hockey is its breath and most fundamental store of energy.

One school of thought regarding hockey's origins maintains that it all began when the French explorers lived among the Indians in northern North America. Seemingly, the French observed an exciting game in which the Indians organized themselves in two teams, each defending a goal at opposite ends of a rectangular field. Teammates used sticks with curved ends to shoot a ball down the field into the opposing team's goal. Proponents of this view report that the French named the game after their word for a shepherd's crook, *hocquet.*

Other hockey history buffs argue that hockey has its roots in similar European field games enjoyed in England, France, and Holland over five hundred years ago. Nonetheless, four Canadian cities—Windsor, Nova Scotia; Kingston, Ontario; Halifax, Nova Scotia; and Montreal, Quebec—each claim to be the site where hockey first developed. According to the Hockey Hall of Fame (HHOF), Thomas Chandler Haliburton of Windsor wrote about the game in 1844 in his memoirs, referring to "hurley," a frozen-pond game of his childhood, which is similar to the game that would later be known as "hockey." Accordingly, therefore, hockey's namesake may have nothing to do with French. A certain Colonel Hockey was an officer stationed at Windsor's Fort Edward during the 1880s. Legend has it that his workout regimen for his troops included playing hurley, which was dubbed "Hockey's Game."

Some hockey history buffs contend that playing according to rules similar to the field game the Indians played, but on the ice, may indeed have been the innovation of a group of British soldiers during the mid-nineteenth century. The earliest known recorded account of the first real, official, organized competition occurred among four soldier teams in Kingston, Ontario, in 1855. Later records tell us that soldiers stationed in Halifax, Nova Scotia, conducted tournaments in the 1870s. However, these competitions included dozens of players to a side, according to the HHOF. During the mid-nineteenth century, the game apparently had several names, in addition to hurley; it was also known as wicket, ricket, and break-shins.

The first ice hockey game with few players to a side was, according to early records, the invention of James Creighton, a native of Halifax, who introduced the game in Montreal around 1873. He developed the "Halifax Rules," featuring nine players to a side. The game became widely popular in Montreal thereafter. According to the HHOF, W. F. Robertson, a McGill University student and one of Montreal's earliest hockey enthusiasts, organized the game with fifteen players to a side. Players skated after a lacrosse ball with its rounded edges cut off—a square puck. HHOL records indicate that, by the end of the 1880s, hockey had become a popular game throughout Ontario as well. By the turn of the century, young people throughout Canada were participating in the sport.

When a team showed up at the Montreal Winter Carnival two men short, competition began between seven-player teams. The norm that cemented itself to the sport sometime during the 1880s was for sides to consist of two defensemen, three forwards, one rover, and one goalie. In 1893 the prize of the Stanley Cup was created, named after Lord Stanley of Preston, governor of Canada at that time, who donated a large silver cup to the best team in Canada. Teams battled to secure the trophy for themselves, as there was no higher prize for ice hockey excellence. The cup remains the sport's most prestigious tangible reward—awarded to the champion team of the National Hockey League (NHL).

The International Pro Hockey League, organized in 1904 and based in Michigan's Upper Peninsula, was the first professional hockey league. Its existence was important historically since it established regulations in professional play. By 1909 the league collapsed. The National Hockey Association (NHA) then emerged and firmly established the fundamental rules of the game, though certain regulations were altered later as needed.

Not long after the NHA was organized, the Pacific Coast Hockey Association (PCHA) took root. By 1914 the two leagues sent their finest teams to compete in an NHA versus PCHA series competition. The goal was to win Lord Stanley's Cup. As World War I interfered with continued success for the NHA and PCHA, a new league was organized by the end of the war—the National Hockey League (NHL), which first included the following clubs: Montreal Canadiens,

Montreal Wanderers, Ottawa Senators, Quebec Bulldogs, and Toronto Arenas. Following the guidelines set by the NHA a short time before, the NHL dropped the rover position. The NHA folded, and in 1918 the NHL and PCHA competed for the Stanley Cup: the Toronto Arenas beat the PCHA's Vancouver Millionaires in a five-game series, three to two. By the mid-1920s the PCHA had dissolved. In 1926, the NHL was the prevailing professional league, which included six franchises in Canada and the United States: the Boston Bruins, the Detroit Red Wings, the Chicago Blackhawks, the New York Rangers, the Toronto Maple Leafs, and the Montreal Canadiens. These teams later became known as the NHL's "original six."

During the twentieth century, recreational and locally run league ice hockey became increasingly more popular on ponds and rinks across Canada and the United States. By the mid-1970s, ice hockey earned distinction as the second most popular game worldwide after soccer. In 1973, Eveleth, Minnesota, began housing the U.S. Hockey Hall of Fame. Still, ice hockey was viewed among North Americans as largely a Canadian sport, and players throughout the NHL by and large were Canadian nationals. In 1972 Team Canada (made up of NHL players) played in the Summit Series against the Soviet Union's world champion team. Team Canada defeated the Soviet team when Canada's Paul Henderson scored a memorable goal in the final minute of the final game.

In 1967, the NHL underwent big changes with reorganization to a two-division expanded league of twelve teams. The increased international appeal of the game led to the creation of the World Hockey Association in 1972, which signed a few defectors from the NHL, including those most talked-about, Bobby Hull and Gordie Howe. In 1979, the WHA folded with several of its teams moving to the NHL, including the New England (later Hartford, then Carolina Hurricanes) Whalers and the Edmonton Oilers. Twenty years later, rumor had it that the WHA might reemerge, in light of the

2004–05 NHL players' strike and consequent lockout. Meanwhile, hockey fans enjoyed attending more college games at NHL venues, as well as viewing junior-level and minor-league competitions at area arenas. In July of 2005, the NHL players' union and franchise owners settled the strike.

The 1980 "Miracle on Ice" Team USA win drew many new American fans into hockey. Idolizing the young men of the USA Olympic hockey team, American youngsters took to the ice more than ever. *Sports Illustrated* called the event perhaps "the single most indelible moment in all of U.S. sports history." NCAA coach Herb Brooks had led the team to defeat the "red machine" from the Soviet Union in Lake Placid on February 22, 1980, in the Olympic semi-playoffs. Team USA then beat Finland two days later in the finals to bring home the gold. The victory of the American underdog team against Communism's Soviets during the Cold War transcended sports to affect America's political and cultural psyche, as the weary United States had just endured during the previous decade defeat in Vietnam, the Watergate scandal, a recession, an energy crisis, and was facing fifty-two of its own held hostage in Iran and the ongoing, pervasive threat of

Jim Craig, Goalie for the U.S. "Miracle on Ice" Olympic Team, suffered the death of his mother only months before helping the U.S. win gold. One of the most heart-warming images of the 1980 Olympics was that of Craig, draped in an American flag, searching the Lake Placid crowd for his father, asking, "Where's my father?"

Photo credit: Hockey Hall of Fame

Soviet military might. Americans embraced this Olympic miracle energetically and frantically. Hockey had proved to be a tool of hope, and American hockey would never be the same. The 10,490 registered American hockey teams of 1980 increased to 14,969 by 1990. By 1997, USA Hockey registered 29,479 teams, and the numbers have continued to increase. In 2003–04, USA Hockey had 535,439 registered ice and in-line players, coaches, and officials.

Traditionally, amateur ice hockey has been more popular and best supported in Michigan, Minnesota, North Dakota, Wisconsin, Colorado, New England, and, of course, throughout Canada. Slowly, with expansion teams rapidly sprouting in warmer regions of the United States, young players in places like Tampa, Florida; San Jose, California; Phoenix, Arizona; and Nashville, Tennessee, are beginning to enjoy ice hockey. The local leagues that have sprung up for youth and junior players in the United States have been unified under a set of rules and guidelines established by USA Hockey, originally founded in 1937 as the Amateur Hockey Association of the United States (AHAUS). Part of the larger International Ice Hockey Federation, USA Hockey, headquartered in Colorado Springs, Colorado, is the formal governing organization for American ice hockey leagues and programs and sponsors the U.S. Olympic team. Hockey Canada is the lead organization for youth hockey in Canada.

A SAMPLING OF ICE HOCKEY'S GREATS

An examination of the lives of some of ice hockey's greatest players will offer insight into the game's play dynamics and spirit. A look at ice hockey's notables can help you understand your son's or daughter's development as a player on the ice, a student to a coach, and a member of a team. Below are snapshot biographies of a few of ice hockey's best forwards, its most creative defenseman, and two innovative goalies.

Carefully note, Mom, these great players' coming-of-age experiences in hockey. They are lessons to pass on to today's young players.

Hockey's "Great One," Wayne Gretzky, is acclaimed by hockey fans for his record-breaking and his modesty.
Photo credit: O-Pee-Chee/Hockey Hall of Fame

Wayne Gretzky was booed for playing too well. Fifteen-year-old Gordie Howe had a disappointing experience with the New York Rangers. Guy Lafleur's skating was called "pretty." An insightful, wise youth coach turned Bobby Orr into hockey's greatest defenseman. Jacques Plante took a stand for safety in the net. Despite being plagued with poor health since childhood, Maurice Richard was arguably the NHL's most relentless and most driven goal scorer. Patrick Roy was driven even as a child to transform himself from an average net player into the NHL's greatest goalie.

The Great One—Wayne Gretzky

I approach each game as if I were still a kid, wishing that one day I would play in the NHL. I play each game knowing that every kid would love to be in my position."
—Wayne Gretzky, in *Sports Illustrated for Kids*

Hockey great Phil Esposito once remarked that Gretzky's hockey instinct could only be from God. At five feet eleven inches and 165 pounds, Gretzky was not born with overtly physical gifts. He was never the strongest or the fastest player on the teams he played with. He was arguably the most creative, the smartest, and the most modest. Ironically, this outstanding athlete known for his humility, superior sportsmanship, and team play will forever be labeled "The Great One."

Gretzky's creative offensive play dominated 1980s hockey, presenting a new angle of the game, one featuring intelligent, skillful offensive maneuvering and deemphasizing defensive bullying tactics. Gretzky's style stressed active play over reactive.

Born on January 26, 1961, in Brantford, Ontario, Wayne Gretzky was the oldest of five children. His father, a telephone company employee, put young Wayne in skates as a toddler. He could skate by age two and a half. It wasn't long before Gretzky's father taught him hockey skills, noting early on his son's special athletic talent and heart. As a child, Gretzky also played baseball, football, lacrosse, and soccer—his favorite being baseball. Gretzky adored hockey as well, studying and admiring his favorite player, Gordie Howe, whose jersey he wore as much as his parents would allow him.

Heeding the advice of his father to "skate to where the puck is going, not to where it has been," Gretzky performed at the top end of his level early on. Canadian youth hockey observers recognized Gretzky as a prodigy hockey player by the time he was six. As an adult, Gretzky admitted to journalists that he had always felt as if he were on display, and it wasn't easy. Though at age ten he was applauded for scoring 378 goals with the Brantford Nadrofsky Steelers and was even asked to sign autographs, the parents of opposing teams also loudly booed him. This kind of pressure forced Gretzky to move to Toronto at age fourteen. The following year, he was the subject of a Canadian television show. At seventeen, still in high school, Gretzky signed with the WHA's Indianapolis Racers, but did not actually play for the team, which went bankrupt and sold Gretzky to the Edmonton Oilers. After one season, the WHA went under and the NHL absorbed Edmonton.

From 1980 to 1988, Gretzky scored 583 goals and tallied 1,036 assists for Edmonton. He won eight Most Valuable Player awards and led his team as captain to win four Stanley Cup championships before being traded to the L.A. Kings. During his first season with L.A., Gretzky scored fifty-four times and contributed 114 assists. On October 15, 1989, he beat Howe's record of 1,850 career points. After nearly eight seasons with L.A., Gretzky became a free agent with the St. Louis Blues, playing with personal friend Brett Hull. After losing a seven-game double-overtime playoff heartbreaker to the Detroit Red Wings, Gretzky signed with the New York Rangers, joining former Edmonton Oilers' teammate Mark Messier. After three years with New York, Gretzky, number ninety-nine, retired from playing professional hockey in the spring of 1999. Gretzky was inducted into the Hockey Hall of Fame the following November. He ended two decades of professional playing holding sixty-one NHL records, including 894 NHL career goals and 2,857 points. He was the NHL's regular season MVP nine times and playoff MVP two times. In 2006, he was named head coach of the Coyotes.

Gretzky continued with hockey as minority owner of the Phoenix Coyotes and executive director for the 2002 Olympic champion Team Canada. Gretzky also pursued numerous spokesperson opportunities for charity and for profit. Known for his kindness to children, cheerfully giving away autographs and sticks to young fans, Gretzky was able to enjoy spending more time with his own children he had with former actress Janet Jones, whom he married in July of 1988. His children are Pauline, Emma, Ty, Robert, and Trevor.

Mr. Hockey—Gordie Howe

At Detroit's Joe Louis Arena, home of the Red Wings, an image of a young number nine is displayed with this message: "This is the foundation that gets moms and dads out of bed on dark, cold winter mornings so their sons or daughters can skate. And the dream is always the same: Maybe my kid will be the next Gordie Howe."

Indeed, many, including Wayne Gretzky, argue that Howe is the greatest hockey player ever. He certainly is the most enduring and durable, having skated thirty-two professional seasons to retire at age fifty-two.

Born in 1928 in Saskatchewan, Canada, Howe was the fifth of nine children born to a laborer who struggled to feed his large family during the Depression. Howe snagged his first pair of skates from

The Three Howes. In 1973, shortly after retiring from the NHL, Gordie Howe (center) joined sons Mark (right) and Marty (left) to play for the new WHA's Houston Aeros. Hockey mom and wife, Colleen Howe, negotiated the Howe contracts as their agent, an unprecedented undertaking for a woman in the world of professional hockey.
Photo credit: O-Pee-Chee/Hockey Hall of Fame

a bag of secondhand items his mother purchased for fifty cents. He was five years old. From then on, Howe skated every chance he got. A big boy who worked construction with his father, Howe developed into a strong and talented skater. At fifteen, Howe was six-feet-tall and two hundred pounds, a notably large frame for a man in the 1940s. About that time, the New York Rangers invited Howe to try-out camp. He did not make the cut.

The following year, Howe tried out for and made the Detroit Red Wings. As a seventeen-year-old, Howe played on the Wing's minor team. After a superb season, Red Wings' management sent him to play on its major team. Howe impressed fans and commentators right from the start, during his first major-league game. It wasn't long until Red Wings' coach Tommy Ivan created "the Production Line," which included Howe on right wing, Ted Lindsey on left wing, and Sid Abel at center. The line worked as one formidable attacking line that dominated the NHL, earning the Red Wings four Stanley Cup championships.

Playing what Howe dubbed "religious hockey: it's better to give than to receive," Howe was reputedly a thoroughly antagonistic and physical player. Even his son Mark admitted that his dad was "mean" on the ice. Nonetheless, this hockey warrior is on record as claiming that before each game he prayed that no one would get hurt.

Howe himself was badly hurt during a playoff game against the Toronto Maple Leafs, suffering a severe blow into the boards. Twenty-one-year-old Howe was out for the rest of the 1950 playoffs with a fractured skull. Though fans feared he would be out for good, he returned the next fall for another season of top-end goal scoring.

Howe may have been mean on the ice, but off the ice he was known as quiet and kind. After Howe's wife, Colleen, later known as "Mrs. Hockey," discovered that he was being paid far less than much lesser NHL players, she took over as her husband's agent, the first female agent for a pro player. She demanded fair compensation for her husband and payment for pre- and post-retirement appearances for NHL promotional events.

Mrs. Hockey negotiated a deal that brought Howe out of retirement from the NHL at age forty-five. He joined two of his four children, Marty and Mark, also agented by Mrs. Howe, to play for the WHA's Houston Aeros. Howe led his team to the WHA championship that first season with the Aeros, having made 100 points and winning the Most Valuable Player award. In 1977, Colleen Howe struck a deal to move her husband and sons to the New England Whalers. Fifteen WHA goals were recorded as scored by Howe with an assist by Howe and another assist by Howe. After the NHL absorbed the Whalers, Howe shared a line with Bobby Hull and Dave Keon, which became known as the "Three Old Goats." Though the combined age of the three forwards was 130, the line was strong and swift.

In 1991, Howe and other hockey veterans filed a lawsuit against the NHL for misappropriating $27 million of their pension fund. Howe reportedly earned an annual pension of about $15,000 after having skated twenty-six seasons with the NHL.

In September of 1997, Howe played the season opener of the International Hockey League's Detroit Vipers to make him the only hockey player to play professionally during six consecutive decades. He was sixty-nine.

The Dazzling Flower—Guy Lafleur

Translated from French as "the flower," Guy Lafleur's surname suits his skating. It was called beautiful, flowing, creative. Not only was Lafleur's skating quick and skilled, it was pretty. Even when Lafleur's shots failed, fans were dazzled. They loved to watch him skate.

The Montreal Canadiens drafted Lafleur in 1971. He had been a well-known junior player with the Quebec Ramparts, finishing his last season with 130 goals and 79 assists. Montreal fans expected Lafleur to fill the void left by Jean Béliveau, whose jersey, number four, was offered to Lafleur. Insightfully, Lafleur turned down the jersey.

Lafleur would not try to be Béliveau, but nonetheless, he became the largest box-office draw for Montreal with six consecutive fifty-goal and one-hundred-point seasons. In 1983, Lafleur passed the coveted five hundred-goal mark. He retired from Montreal in 1985 with three Art Ross trophies and five Stanley Cups.

Lafleur's last year with Montreal was difficult, however. Coach Jacques Lemaire's defensive-wall strategy stifled Lafleur's skate. (Lemaire's defensive strategy, by the way, is credited for his Stanley Cup victory in 1995 with the New Jersey Devils.) He had less ice time and fewer opportunities to score. Fans started to turn on him, and he seemed to lose his flash on the ice. After appealing unsuccessfully for a trade from Montreal, Lafleur quit in 1985. In 1988, he returned to the NHL, the same year he was inducted into the Hockey Hall of Fame, playing for the New York Rangers, who added him after a tryout. Though New York did not make the playoffs that year, Lafleur displayed during the season the skating dazzle and dexterity he was known for.

After retiring from the NHL in 1991, Lafleur patched up his relationship with Montreal and accepted an off-ice position and lived in Montreal with his wife, Lise, and sons Martin and Marc.

The Rocket—Maurice Richard

Others could skate faster than Richard. Some could shoot harder and pass better. Nobody, however, approached his intensity. Nobody wanted to win more. Not Gordie Howe, not Gretzky, not Mario Lemieux. Not anybody before his time, or since.

—Red Fisher in *The Montreal Gazette*, May 2000

Maurice "The Rocket" Richard was a right-wing attacker with a left-handed shot. And attack he did. He was a warrior on the ice, ruthlessly charging opponents and bursting toward the puck and crashing the net like a launched rocket. Press clippings of his era record numerous accounts by Richard's opponents who fell victim to his tactics and testified to what one paper headlined as "the Rocket's Red Glare"—Richard's piercing eyes. He was the NHL's toughest, a remarkable reputation for a player who had had to endure poor health since childhood, specifically a problem with brittle bones.

He was born Joseph Henri Maurice Richard on August 4, 1921, the second oldest of seven children, to Onésime, a carpenter, and Alice Richard. Young Richard spent the greater part of his childhood in the Nouveau Bordeaux district of Montreal, playing on the Rivières-des-Prairies and on nearby ponds. He started playing organized youth hockey at age eleven. As a teen, Richard trained to become a machinist despite his heart's cry to play pro hockey.

He played in the juniors from 1938 to 1942, during which his weak bones suffered many breaks and fractures, mostly in his ankles and wrists. He broke his ankle sixteen times before his debut in the NHL with the Montreal Canadiens on October 31, 1942. The Rocket stayed with his home team for his entire NHL career, playing eighteen seasons and shooting 544 goals, becoming the first NHL player, in 1958, to have 500 career goals. He was also the first player to score fifty goals in one regular season—1944–45. This came after his stellar performance in 1943–44 as part of "the Punch Line" with center Elmer Lach and left wing Hector "Toe" Blake. He locked away thirteen consecutive All-Star contests and led the NHL in scoring five times. He enjoyed eight Stanley Cup championships.

Richard's wild temper on and off the ice got him into trouble frequently with NHL president Clarence Campbell who fined him regularly. Some of Richard's wealthier fans paid the fines for him.

Then came the last straw for Campbell. Richard went too far in the third period of a game against the Boston Bruins in 1955. After being struck in the head by the stick of Bruin Hal Laycoe, Richard retaliated heavily. During the ensuing fight, Richard jacked a linesman twice. Laycoe wound up with a five-minute penalty for the original high-sticking infraction that set Richard off. Richard was sent to the locker room with a match penalty. Later, Campbell suspended Richard for the duration of the regular season and the playoffs.

The suspension enraged Montreal fans. Shortly after the incident, Campbell showed up to watch Montreal take on the Red Wings at home. Fans threw objects at him, chanted, and began a protest that led to French Quebec nationalistic rioting in the streets of Montreal. Richard, who sought to stay out of politics, found that his celebrity had emerged into an image that Francophones hoisted as a symbol of the determination of the Quebecois who wished to secede from Canada. During the second day of rioting, Richard spoke to fans in a radio broadcast, convincing protesters to go home.

Richard played the following season with a new teammate who was dear to him, his brother Henri, dubbed "The Pocket Rocket," who was fifteen years his junior. Richard later suffered a number of injuries beginning with an Achilles' tendon partially severed by the skate of Toronto Maple Leaf Marc Reaume on November 13, 1957. He retired in 1960. He was then able to spend more time with his wife, Lucille, and their three sons and two daughters and enjoyed fishing as much as he could. He did some work in Montreal's front office and ran a small fishing-line business from his home.

On May 27, 2000, The Rocket died from abdominal cancer. His death, like his suspension, moved many Canadian Francophones to tears of Quebecois pride and hope. Richard was their icon. For them, The Rocket was bigger than life.

The Prodigy Defenseman—Bobby Orr

At age eleven, Bobby Orr's Parry Sound, Ontario, coach, Bucko McDonald, put him on defense for the first time. Orr had previously played forward, like his dad, Doug Orr, and proved himself even as a small boy as a gifted stick handler with a powerful shot. McDonald's keen hockey-sense eye detected Orr's uniqueness as a player—particularly the speed that would make him a formidable defenseman.

The Boston Bruins franchise had its sights on Orr while he was still in his early teens. The Ontario Hockey League Oshawa Generals made a special allowance to play the fourteen-year-old Orr. Orr's parents drove him from Ontario to the games. He did not practice with the team. Nonetheless, he showed prowess and was selected for the Second All-Star team. For three years, Orr dominated junior hockey while Boston waited for him to turn of age. Finally in 1966 Orr, reputed among Boston fans as an ice hockey prodigy, joined the Bruins. Fans attended Bruins games just to watch the rookie. Boston coach Harry Sinden remarked on the start of Orr's play with the Bruins saying, "We played him at center six of seven games in his rookie year. He was only tremendous. On defense, he was phenomenal." Orr set scoring records while playing defense. His offensive play rivaled that of forward prodigies like Wayne Gretzky and Mario Lemieux; he was a defenseman who led the league in assists five times. Recognized as a superior defender who also created scoring opportunities, Orr won the Norris Trophy eight years in a row as the NHL's best blue-line player.

Orr very rarely dropped his gloves to fight. A defenseman not known for fighting, fans praised Orr for his uncanny ability to gauge the speed of the player he passed to in creating scoring chances. Orr-era hockey fans will recall the image of Orr's goal at the close of the final game that "sweeped" the 1970 Stanley Cup win for the Bruins. It is a snapshot of Orr thrown into midair by a St. Louis player—hands and stick raised in celebration.

Fans will also sadly remember Orr's betrayal by his agent and the knee injuries that led to him leaving Boston to play with the Blackhawks as a free agent. When Orr's knees finally did him in, he was forced to retire at age thirty. Gordie Howe said of Orr's early retirement, "Losing Bobby was the biggest blow the NHL has ever suffered."

Free-Thinking Goalie—Jacques Plante

Jacques Plante popularized a hockey gear innovation moms highly value—the mask. Plante was not the first goalie to wear a mask. That was Clint Benedict in 1930. It was a padded, leather mask that failed to protect him from a nose break that precipitated Benedict's retirement. Plante was, nonetheless, the first goalie to insist on wearing a mask and the first to wear masks made of materials with better protective potential than leather.

On November 2, 1959, Plante was hit in the nose with a puck. In the locker room, he insisted to Montreal Canadiens' coach Tom Blake, who believed mask-wearing impaired performance, that he either wear the mask (he had been using in practices) in the net or he would quit. Blake agreed to allow the mask in games until Plante's nose healed. But the mask stayed for the duration of Plante's net career.

Observers ridiculed Plante's mask-wearing as cowardly, but Plante did not care. Nor was he embarrassed to knit in public. And he ignored criticism of how he frequently stayed at different hotels from those of his team. An asthmatic, Plante demanded particular requirements for air quality.

Plante felt vindicated in his mask-wearing after a hit he took just above the eye during the 1970 Stanley Cup finals. He suffered a concussion, but no cut or fracture. Plante maintained that the mask had saved his life.

Though he was thoroughly independent and private, Plante was a skilled goalie whose play was motivated by team spirit. He was known to call out directions to teammates from the net and was the first goalie to signal icing for his defensemen. His roaming from the crease to play the puck was innovative. He said that he had to play the net that way because as a kid he had played with defensemen who were poor skaters. Nonetheless, his roaming tactics were adopted by a number of goalies after him.

Plante left the Montreal Canadiens in 1963 for the New York Rangers. He retired in 1965, but returned to the NHL to play for the St. Louis Blues in 1968. He left hockey for good in 1975 after playing for Toronto, Boston, and Edmonton. Plante walked away with five Stanley Cups and six Vezina trophies. He died of cancer in 1986.

The Goose—Patrick Roy

This superstitious, neck-flexing goalie was reputed to be arrogant in the sports press. More likely, reporters misread his resolve and confidence, which Roy considered critical for success in defending the net, as smugness. What's more is that the French-speaking Roy struggled with the English language during most of his NHL career, which probably contributed to his being misunderstood by the Anglophone press and fans. Because he was the greatest pressure goalie in the NHL, Roy's superstitious avoidance of skating on the ice's red and blue lines and his "talking to the goalposts" endeared him to fans instead of annoying them with his eccentricities. But then again, an eccentric goalie is nothing out of the ordinary in hockey.

Roy came from an athletic family. His dad had been scouted by the Brooklyn Dodgers as a young man. His mother had been a competitive synchronized swimmer. His brother, Stephane, would be drafted by the NHL in 1985 (a year after Roy) to play for the Minnesota North Stars.

As a kid, Roy was an average player who cheered for the Quebec Nordiques and dreamed of playing net in the NHL. He began as a player at age six. After relieving his team's injured goalie, he was hooked on playing goalie. By age seven, he was determined to pursue goaltending all the way to the NHL. As an adult, Roy would later admit to being enamored with the position as a seven-year-old because of the cool padding goalies wore. He also wanted to impress his grandmother, an intense hockey fan who adored goalie living legend Ken Dryden.

Roy worked hard to bring his skills from average to great. In 1982 he dropped out of high school in eleventh grade to play in the juniors, for the Granby Bisons. With a 45–54 first-season record, averaging 5.32 goals against, Roy became Quebec's Junior League's best goaltender. In 1984, the Montreal Canadiens drafted him and sent him to the minors to train with goalie coach François Allaire, who would remain Roy's coach for the remainder of his professional hockey career.

Roy came to the NHL driven and determined, playing for the Canadiens barely out of his teens. He was the youngest to win the Conn Smythe Trophy in 1985 at age twenty. Roy's boyhood NHL dream of playing with the Nordiques would be realized after a rather low game in his career. On December 2, 1995, Roy was in the Montreal Canadiens net in a 9–1 deficit against the Detroit Red Wings. Canadiens' rookie coach Mario Tremblay pulled Roy out well beyond the point of no return. The goalie was furious. He stormed off the ice directly to Canadiens' president Ronald Corey, who was seated behind the bench. Roy declared that he was quitting the team. Four days later, he was traded to the brand new Colorado Avalanche, formerly Roy's beloved Nordiques. Roy was happy and performed spectacularly for the Avs. Against the Canadiens, he stopped thirty-seven out of thirty-nine shots for a 5–2 win. Colorado coach Marc Crawford claimed that the addition of Roy was the final touch to a champion team. The prediction would prove to be on the mark.

In the Stanley Cup finals against the Florida Panthers, Roy found that his net was the target of Panthers fans throwing plastic rats after each Panthers goal. Roy did not seek shelter in the net. He skated his crease ignoring the spray of falling rats. Finally, he skated to the Colorado bench and declared, "No more rats." Not another puck went by him in the series. The Avs swept the Panthers with ripple overtime in game four.

Roy retired in 2003 as the NHL's greatest pressure goalie and with the record for the most playoff victories, the most playoff games, the most playoff shutouts, the most minutes played, and the most thirty-win seasons. In 1993, he had led the Canadiens to the Stanley Cup with ten consecutive overtime wins. He collected four Stanley Cup rings, three Conn Sythe trophies, three Vezina trophies, and a William M. Jennings award.

Roy's unique contribution to hockey goaltending was his method of covering the bottom half of the net. It became the standard for young goalies. He also brought a new athleticism to the position, believing that the goalie is the sixth position player, the third defenseman.

FUN FACTS

- Hockey became an Olympic event in 1920.
- The nickname for the Montreal Canadiens, the Habs, resulted from a misunderstanding of their logo—a C wrapped around an H for "Club de Hockey Canadien." In 1924, someone erroneously told Madison Square Garden owner Tex Rickard that the H stood for *habitant,* a colloquialism for Quebec farmers. Rickard believed that the players predominantly came from the farms and were therefore called the Habs.
- The first U.S.-born NHL player was Billy Burch. He was born in Yonkers, New York, in 1900.

- Gordie and Colleen Howe named their teacup poodle Rocket, after Gordie's on-ice nemesis, Maurice "The Rocket" Richard.
- Manon Rheaume became the first woman to play in the NHL when she goaltended for the Tampa Bay Lightning during a preseason game on September 23, 1992.
- Many youth players feel lucky to be handed a jersey carrying the number nine. Others prefer four, Bobby Orr's and Jean Béliveau's number. Nine is the number Maurice Richard retired from Montreal, Gordie Howe retired from Detroit, and Bobby Hull retired from Hartford. Other great number nines include Paul Kariya, Mike Modano, and Johnny Bucyk. Steve Yzerman and Joe Sakic wear number nineteen, and Sergey Federov wears ninety-one. Wayne Gretzky wore ninety-nine in tribute to his childhood idol Howe and retired the number from the NHL. Recognizing Gretzky as hockey's "Great One," Mario Lemieux chose for himself ninety-nine upside down—sixty-six.

Hextall

Three generations of Hextalls have played in the NHL. Hall of Famer Bryan played twelve years with the New York Rangers, 1936–48. Sons Bryan Jr. and Dennis also played in the NHL. Bryan Jr.'s son Ron, a talented goalie, finished his career with the Philadelphia Flyers in 1997. In 2001, he too was granted Hall-of-Famer distinction. "Hextall" adorned the back of at least one NHL jersey during more than thirty seasons.

Howe

Mr. Hockey, Gordie Howe, in 1979–80, his thirty-second year of pro hockey, played in the WHA with sons Mark and Marty. Several WHA goals were recorded as scored by Howe with assists by Howe

Here is Colleen Howe as a young hockey mom signing autographs for young players at Detroit's Olympia Arena. Photo credit: the Howe family

and Howe. Imagine the delight of Mrs. Hockey!

Colleen J. Howe, Mrs. Hockey, is the ultimate hockey mom. Not only was she active in the world of pro hockey as the wife of hockey legend Gordie Howe, she was important to the development of youth hockey, spearheading the emergence of new youth-hockey schools and programs in the Metro Detroit area, where she and Mr. Howe resided. She also founded the Detroit Junior Red Wings, the first Junior A team in the United States and negotiated the pro contracts for her husband and sons Marty and Mark. Working tirelessly for charitable efforts, Mrs. Howe established the Howe Foundation; her commitment in helping people is as legendary among Detroiters as her dedication to her hockey players. For her work in hockey, Mrs. Howe is distinguished as a U.S. Hockey Hall of Famer. In addition, she is namesake to the Gordie and Colleen Howe Middle School in Abbotsford, British Columbia, and the Colleen J. Howe Ice Arena in Sandusky, Michigan, Mrs. Howe's birthplace.

Angela Ruggiero

Equally delighted must have been the parents of Angela and Bill Ruggiero. In 2005, Angela joined the Central Hockey League Tulsa Oilers to become the first woman position player and second woman in the league. On January 28, Angela defended brother Bill's net. Before playing with the Oilers, Angela won gold and silver Olympic medals as part of the U.S. Women's National Team and played in five International Ice Hockey Federation championships. After playing four years of NCAA Division I hockey at Harvard, Angela was honored with the Patty Kazmaier Memorial Award for being at the top of her game.

Abby Hoffman

When Abby Hoffman played in the Toronto Hockey League in the 1950s, most fans were unaware that she was a woman. She pioneered female participation in hockey as she shined on defense. Her influence in women's hockey was officially recognized when the first Abby Hoffman Cup was presented in 1982.

Foster Hewitt

Foster Hewitt is hockey's most famous broadcaster. He delivered the most quotable commentary in the history of the game. "He shoots, he scores!" was his creation. So was his quirky introduction from the Maple Leafs broadcast booth: "Hello hockey fans in Canada and the United States and Newfoundland." True old-time hockey fans know the story and significance behind Hewitt's words the moment Team Canada beat the Soviet Union's team in the Summit Series on September 28, 1972: "Henderson has scored for Canada!"

2

Fan Mom

I have been a hockey mom for a long time. Long gone are the days when I had to explain what is worn where, why there are three lines on the ice, what the goalie's crease is, the referee's crease, the penalty box, icing, off-sides, or a myriad of other things. No longer do I have to help little ones tie skates or put on those awkward pieces of equipment. Gone, too, are the days when a good laugh could be had from watching my youngsters cross the blue line while the puck stayed behind. Now I look out on the ice and expect to see a child who knows when to cross the blue line, when to move the puck back to the defenseman, when it's appropriate to take the body or the shot or, for that matter, the penalty. I watch with the same intensity with which I want them to play. Try as I might, I cannot help second-guessing a coach, another player, my son, or a referee. And, while I usually abide by the rules of zero tolerance, I generally banish myself to a far end of the stands where I can mutter to myself and relieve my frustrations—sometimes resorting to a quiet chant of, "Hockey is fun, hockey is fun, hockey is fun!" But mostly, I must admit, it is not as much fun as it was when the boys were little . . . You can no longer come to watch your child perfect one newly acquired skill—like skating! Instead, you come to watch your child participate in what has become a game that relies on "team."... It is team skills that will be the older player's best asset. And, we parents need to learn those team skills, too. We need to know that our kids are not the only ones on the ice who can put the puck in the net. Sure it's impossible not to be subjective when it comes to our children . . . but we can try. And, if we want to survive throughout our children's hockey careers, we must do it. Just remember, "Hockey is fun, hockey is fun, hockey is fun!"

—Pat Markham, Hockey Mom feature writer for *Hockey Stop,* a youth hockey publication in Illinois and Missouri.

ce hockey includes wonderful ingredients for thrilling entertainment: skillful skating and stickhandling, slick passing and shooting, and speed and coordination in moving around the rink. You're amazed at how such young people can move and balance themselves

Mite teams pursue control of the puck.   *Photo by Andrew Doig*

across ice while handling a small object with a narrow stick. Even if you've never skated before, you can appreciate the skills required to play such a game. I've found that there is only one thing that can take the fun out of it for me as I watch my sons play hockey. It's not losing, though losing's not exactly fun. It's ugly behavior by hockey parents. And this is the number one problem in youth hockey.

HEADS-UP HOCKEY PARENTING

A wise friend of mine has a great saying for times of frustration and potential confrontation: "Keep your poise and rise above the noise." These are words to live by at the rink. As a rookie hockey mom, you are bound to witness other rink parents behaving abominably. There is no way to avoid feeling emotional about a game and about your child's experience at the rink. Even the most seemingly mild-mannered moms and dads can turn into ugly monsters on game day. These monsters unfortunately might take away the fun of hockey for other parents, and most despicably, for the child players. It's regrettable, it's ugly, but it's a pervasive reality in youth hockey today.

Deflect it with what I call "heads-up hockey parenting." As your child heeds to his coach's instruction to skate heads up, enforcing good play and preventing spinal injury, so should you, Mom, heed to the voice ringing in your conscience that reminds you, "Heads up." If you keep your head up, looking to your target—a positive hockey experience for your child— you will steer clear of most potential entanglements with other parents. If you're checked, however, and chances are you will be at least once in a while by some unreasonable parent, skate through it with your head up. Deflect the behavior, shake it off, without allowing it to hurt you or the player you're protecting. Take my friend's saying as a personal anthem for your child and a mandate for yourself. It is not trite to follow the clichéd vow of not "stooping to that level." Stooping is heads-down—dangerous and foolish. Any reasonable veteran hockey mom will tell you that parenting heads up is essential and practical. Think about it; you'll likely associate with these people for years down the road. You can survive with more ease and more fun by keeping your head up and emotions in check.

USA Hockey supports you. The national youth- and amateur-hockey body issued guidelines for a Zero Tolerance Policy, calling for the removal of parents who yell to players, coaches, or refs and linesmen from the glass or stands. State youth hockey organizations have adopted the guidelines, and many rinks have set the policy in motion. I have personally seen boisterous parents removed from my home ice. Hopefully, your league administrators police the parents at your rink, too. If they do not, talk to your division representative or bring the issue up with the league board.

In 2004, Minnesota Hockey took USA Hockey's Zero Tolerance guidelines further and adopted what University of Minnesota head coach Don Lucia dubbed a "fun-at-all-costs" campaign through its Hockey Education Program (HEP). Developed with the help of the Mayo Clinic Sports Medicine Center and the NHL's Minnesota Wild, the program stresses hockey-skills appreciation and fair play. It sets appropriate practice-to-game ratios for levels and rewards teams for good sportsmanship by issuing "fair-play" points that are tallied with

Relax, it's just a game.

scores and wins in league standings. If HEP overflows to other youth hockey organizations, you will be able to tell your young player, "Good sportsmanship matters," with more weight behind you than before.

MODELING HOCKEY-MOM SPORTSMANSHIP TO YOUR CHILD

In youth sports, involvement can creep into over-involvement. Let me state the obvious for a moment: Mom feels good when her child wins; Mom feels bad when her child loses. The key word is "feels." Feelings can sweep you away and drop you out of reality. And reality is that hockey is a *game*, youth hockey is played by *children*, and children are supposed to be having *fun* when they play a game. The satirical play *Round Robin: The Battle of the Hockey Moms* written by Newfoundland native Robert Chafe is sadly based on real rink absurdities. For too many real hockey moms, viewing the caricature-like personalities of this play is like looking in the mirror or walking into their home ice rink. The play underscores how ridiculous a hockey mom could become if she lets her inner fan consume her rational mind.

Looking at the positive, youth hockey is an ideal environment for you to model and encourage self-control. Because the world of youth hockey is imperfect, think of your rink as a microcosm of the real world. Show your child how one ought to react to the ups and downs of the real world. Children learn a great deal through observation. I think it's important for my boys to see me nodding a "hello" or shaking hands with parents on the opposing team. Not only does this ease any tension between the two sides of the stands, it's a signal to my boys of how to show respect to the other team, how to treat my neighbor. Sports psychologist Shane Murphy argues that children learn more from observing adult behavior than from verbal instruction. Always keep in the forefront of your mind that your player is learning from what you don't say as much as what he hears said around him. A child who knows his parent walks away from ugly situations will be a player who skates through and away from the tactics of a bullying player. Add to your good role-modeling by explicitly stressing to your child that, though NHL players are tacitly allowed to fight on the ice, youth hockey is not to be played that way. Tell your player to channel his emotions to his playing, to his skating and stickhandling as opposed to his fists and elbows.

As your child's premier cheerleader, cheer for the team while promoting clean, skills-based hockey. Avoid the ugly "Take him out!" call, which is unfortunately often screamed from the mouths of hockey moms, and keep in mind that screaming directions from the bleachers is not helpful—only annoying—to the spectators around you. Besides, your child on the ice, who is being instructed by his coach, probably can't distinguish the details of your frantic commands anyway, no matter how loudly you yell.

Though you can control how you act, you cannot, of course, control the parents around you who do not choose to exercise self-control and who choose to be poor youth hockey spectators and poor models of good adult behavior. Your child will probably ask you why they act the way they do and say the awful things they say. How do you respond? First, tell your child that, just like skating through a bullying player, he must also tune out the parents at the glass and in the stands. Advise him not to allow them to take the fun out of the game. Second, explain to your child that feelings can cause people to lose their cool. Tell him that when a parent sees his child's team losing and thinks that a call was bad, the parent might speak before thinking. Bullies, whether parents or players, are bullies because of a weakness in their character. They're afraid. Model quiet strength and modest boldness to your child.

BLESS THE HOCKEY MOM

Bless the Hockey Mom who dresses her son,
So he can go have his Six AM fun.
Who loads her pink faced, excited knight,
Into the frosty, metal box in the last blink of night.

Bless the Hockey Mom, who takes the tiny hand,
Of the boy taking steps too quickly towards man.
Who buckles the straps and opens the door,
To a life and journey that's never a chore.

Bless the Hockey Mom who gasps and fears,
As her life starts his battle of smiles and tears.
And who feels the force of her green laser eyes,
As she pushes him faster as the burn fills his thighs.

Bless the Hockey Mom, who screams from her soul,
As the puck trickles softly to the back of the goal.
Whose constant chorus and consistent refrain,
Is effort and fun trumping the score of the game?

Bless the Hockey Mom and her post game phrase,
That doughnuts taste better on cold winter days.
And sticky fingers on a snowy December,
Are the moments and things you'll always remember.

So, Bless the Hockey Mom and her lifelong career,
Of holding you close and loving you near,
Of sacrifice, hugs, commitment and heart,
Of loving a boy, 'till death do they part.

—Reprinted by permission from John Buccigross

THE PARENT TRAP

Shane Murphy, PhD, has written several books about youth-sports parenting. He believes that parents allow their emotions to carry them into what he calls "The Parent Trap," which includes the following:

- "Over-identification"—identifying with your child's playing to the extreme of focusing on your feelings about the results over your child's feelings.
- "Selfish dreaming"—losing sight of your child's desires in your dream for him.
- "Confusing investment with sacrifice"—viewing your time and money spent at the rink as sacrifice as opposed to what it really is: investment in developing your child's character and experience.
- "Competing with other parents"—hoping your child will succeed so much that you find yourself wishing for other children to fail.

There is a list floating around on the Internet called "You know you're a hockey parent when you . . ." If you haven't seen it yet, you'll probably run across it soon. It's very funny. The versions I've seen have no byline attached. My kudos to you, whoever you are. Below I compiled a new, condensed, mom-specific list that includes some variations of points from that list with some new observations of my own.

TOP TEN LIST: HOW TO SPOT A TRUE HOCKEY MOM (BESIDES THE "HOCKEY MOM" DECAL ON HER SUV)

10. She giggles when she overhears other moms rant about how busy soccer is keeping them.
9. As a truck passes, her one-year-old points and distinctly asks, "Zamboni?"
8. She boasted that she was able to do all her Santa-gift shopping in one stop at the local hockey gear store.

7. Her first-grader told his teacher that Thanksgiving is a holiday celebrating the first hockey tournament.

6. She knows that "headman" is a verb.

5. When anyone asks her how old her kids are, she responds with their birth years instead of their ages.

4. During a birthday party competition of carry-the-egg-on-the-spoon, you overheard her describing many of the six-year-olds as, "Good but lack focus." You also overheard her directing them, "Heads up."

3. Her family always heads to a chilly, more northern, climate during school midwinter break, and all of their vacation photos show a tournament banner in the background.

2. You heard her relaying to some other parents the exciting play-by-play of how she "dangled" and "deked" her way to an opening register line at the grocery store.

And the number one way to spot a true hockey mom is . . . (drum roll)

1. Though she often complains about the price of groceries, she defended her purchase of a $150 hockey stick by insisting, "The old one had no goals left in it."

If you don't get these yet, you will by the time you read through this book, certainly by the time you reach the end of your rookie hockey-mom season.

HOCKEY MOM TEN COMMANDMENTS

If a sidelines moral code of conduct were divinely revealed to The Great One himself, I imagine the stone tablets might be inscribed with commandments similar to these:

1. Thou shalt respect the core spirit of the sport of ice hockey—fun.
2. Thou shalt not betray the reputation of the sport with rude, unruly, or self-serving behavior.
3. Thou shalt not lose control of thine emotions and sense of decency.
4. Thou shalt not snub or ridicule the parents or players of the opposing team prior to, during, or following an intense competition.
5. Thou shalt not openly criticize the coaches and officials.
6. Thou shalt in humility and calmness approach other parents, coaches, or administrators with grievances or matters of consequence.
7. Thou shalt not allow thy fan nature to consume thy parenting sense.
8. Thou shalt not scream insults, even when thou hast perceived thine end as the promotion of justice and fairness.
9. Thou shalt not throw things.
10. Thou shalt not conspicuously complain about thy league or division as if to stoke the fire of mob mentality, remembering that thine own judgment may be dead wrong.

The Golden Rule of Youth Hockey

Cheer for all players as thou would have others cheer for thine own.

RINK COURTESY AND ETIQUETTE

- Avoid critiquing play and players out loud. Stifle criticism.
- Steer clear of unreasonable parents looking for confrontation.

- Compliment the officials. Like mothering, it's too often a thankless job.
- Cheer for all children.
- Be friendly to the parents of the opposing team before, during, and after a game.
- Support the fund-raising activities of other teams in your league.
- Stay away from the bench and the glass.
- Avoid blocking play view. In other words, get away from the glass and go to the bleachers. Enter and exit the stands when play has stopped.
- To nurture camaraderie among players, take turns with other parents to treat kids to slushies and bubble-hockey after practices and games.
- Never, never, never criticize the goalie. One thing harder than being a goalie is being a goalie's mom, and she's probably sitting within earshot of you.

If you're one of those people who just gets crazy at sporting events, and you're unsure if you're being a good fan or not, realistically reflect on your behavior at the rink. Look in the mirror. Look around at other parents who act like you do. Do you like what you see? Sure, it's good to have some noise in the stands. Nevertheless, carefully evaluate if you're a mom whom others might be rolling their eyes at. Perhaps your "enthusiasm" causes other parents to sit away from you. If you're unsure, you can ask a mom-friend at the rink whose opinion you respect. You can ask your child!

She might respond, "Mom, you don't know what it's like out there." She just challenged you to start playing yourself. Why not? You can get to really know the game by playing in a women's developmental hockey league in your area. Increasingly more of such leagues are sprouting up. If your rink hasn't organized one yet, then here's a project for you. Put up a flyer and see if there's interest

Roberta Mulder, near in white, of the Westchester (NY) Wildcats B team, moves into action as her teammate Karen Van Den Heuvel and a Stamford Storm opponent look on.

Westchester (NY) Hellcats goaltender Elizabeth Goldman is mom to three boys, Zachary (age 8), Joshua (age 6), and Noah (age 3). Like their mom, Zach and Josh are also goalies.

Photos by Bob Lash, 4 Sons Photography & Digital Imaging

among your league's hockey moms. A great way to acquire hockey awareness and appropriate hockey-fan behavior is to become a recreational hockey player.

DISPLAYING TEAM SPIRIT WITHOUT YELLING
Wear Spirit Scarves

How to make them:

- Purchase heavy fleece corresponding to the colors of your child's team.
- Cut three or four eight-inch-by-sixty-inch pieces.
- Layer the pieces evenly on top of one another, and stitch down the center lengthwise.

- Fringe by shearing straight cuts through the layers from the edge to about three-fourths inch from the center stitch. Fringe widths should be about one to two inches, depending on your preference.

Use Noisemakers

- The cowbell is the traditional noise-making instrument at the rink. Some rinks have banned it, however.
- The air horn is another noisemaker, also banned at some rinks.
- The instrument of pennies or beads in a water bottle is a noisemaker that is permitted at most rinks.

Lisa Procopio (left) of St. Clair Shores, Michigan, and Jennifer Hayes (right) of Bay City, Michigan, sport spirit scarves as part of cheering for their youth players at the Great Lakes Invitational Mites Tournament in Traverse City, Michigan.

Other hockey fan Web sites besides NHL.com and USAHockey.com:

www.exploratorium.edu/hockey—for answers to interesting hockey scientific questions

www.hockeydb.com—for all stats and hockey-card set lists

www.hockeyphreak.com—"Where hockey is everything."—brings news and information to the serious hockey fan www.hockey'sfuture.com—for information on up-and-coming players

www.momsteam.com—provides youth sports information for youth sports moms

www.nhlpa.cpm—for special extra-NHL information on professional players

www.hhof.org—for browsing the archives of hockey history

www.thescec.com/hh—for skills development for players, coaches, and parents

www.uscho.com—for men's and women's college hockey information

www.whockey.com—for the scoop on women's hockey

www.youthhockey.com—includes an active hockey-mom discussion forum

3

Spectator Mom

Some years ago a friend asked me why so much of my time was utilized being active with youth hockey and my reply was, "What better way could I spend my time?" It brought me closer to my youngsters, kept me busy, and gave me gratification and satisfaction . . . I have come to justify my interest in youth hockey completely in my mind. Formerly, as a mother of three boys on teams and a husband in the pro ranks, one might suppose these would be reasons enough. However, none of these seem to be the root of why I have enjoyed going from rink to rink all these years. Instead, I have come to realize some of the real purpose and need for my participation whether large or small.

—Colleen J. Howe, Mrs. Hockey™
www.mrandmrshockey.com/news/news_archived/
colleen_and_youth_hockey.shtml]

HOCKEY RULES
Scoring

The objective of ice hockey is to get the puck into the opponent's net, which means between the goalposts and completely over the red goal line. While keeping his feet outside of the goal's crease—the out-lined area in front of the goal—an attacking player can shoot the puck into the goal. Though his feet cannot cross into the crease while he's shooting, his stick can. A team can also score a goal if the puck deflects into an opponent's net. Since pucks hand-hit or kicked into the net do not count, it is the job of the referee to determine if a puck was deflected off the body of a player or purposefully batted in. A player who scores three goals in a single game is said to have make a hat trick.

Players who make the one or two passes immediately before the puck is shot into the goal get credit in the game's record. This credit is known as an assist. Since the game is a team sport, a good ice hockey coach will stress to youth players that assists are vital to the team's success. Good hockey parenting encourages assists as much as goals. A player who brings in three assists in a single game earns a playmaker distinction. Goals and assists each count for a point in a player's stats. In other words, "two goals and seven points" translates to "two goals and five assists."

Game Duration

The hockey games you watch on television are played in three twenty-minute periods. However, youth players play ten- to fifteen-minute periods, depending on age division. If at the end of the third period the game is tied, your league or tournament rules might call for the contest to continue until a team scores. This type of tie-breaking regulation is known as sudden death overtime. Some leagues handle tie breaking by conducting a shoot-out. If no one scores after a short sudden death period, each team will choose five of its best shooters to position themselves at center ice (the red line). Each player gets a shot on goal. Whichever team has the most suc-cessful shooters—meaning that they shot the puck into the net—wins the game.

Hockey Teams

There is a distinction among all age categories between two kinds of teams: house-league teams; and competitive select or rep teams, called travel teams. A house league takes any child who signs up, placing the best of house on select teams. Representative (travel) teams, more commonly referred to as "rep" teams, hold tryouts to recruit the most skilled players. The competitive travel teams play games more frequently, and they naturally have about double the practices as house, as well as more pressure to win.

Youth ice hockey teams average between fourteen and seventeen players. Ideally a team will have about nine forwards, six defensemen, and one or two goalies (who may also skate out periodically, therefore requiring goalie plus regular player equipment). During a game, six players are out on the ice: the goalie who defends the goal (the net); the defense, two players working to assist the goalie in defending the net, but positioned outside of the goalie's crease; and the forward line, which includes a center, who is usually the guy handling the face-off

Parents and siblings watch a semifinals game at the Michigan State PeeWee B championship tournament. Note the peppy posters hockey moms hung above the stands to rally the strength and determination of the team.

Pictured here are Tanja, Kathie, and Susan, founders of Three Hockey Moms, creators of the original ButtPuck™. It is a puck-shaped seat cushion whose built-in mitt at the back lets it double as a cheering item. See www.sportclix.com/threehockeymoms/ for more information.   *Photo Credit TKTKTKTK*

for his side, and the forward wings, or wingers, one positioned right and one positioned left of the center.

Younger players might skate in predetermined lineups that stick together and do not "change on the fly," or move between the ice and the bench during active play. Older players will skate in varying combinations of forward lines and defensemen. The coach will call new player shifts during play. Shifts last about two to three minutes. In Mini-Mite and Mite levels, some hockey leagues mandate using a buzzer to signal play stoppage for a quick shift change. This is known as "buzzer hockey." Other leagues allow their youngest levels to change on the fly.

Hockey Zones

Five lines run across an ice hockey rink: the red center line, two blue lines, and two red goalie lines. The blue lines divide the ice into three parts: the defensive zone, or the area between a team's goal and the closest blue line; the offensive zone, or the area between the opposing team's goal and their closest blue line; and the neutral zone, or the area between the two blue lines. Some of the shouting you'll hear in the stands related to these zones will be: "Get the puck out of zone," which means get out of a defensive position and get your team closer to the opponent's goal, or a better scoring position; and "Clear the zone," which means get your players out of the offensive zone into neutral so that a skater can get the puck down the ice without committing an offside violation (explained below).

The red dots are where referees can drop the puck for a face-off (explained below). The four dots with the red circles around them are the most common face-off spots, since violations resulting in face-offs usually occur closer to goal. Face-offs that start a game or period occur at the blue dot on the center ice line, enclosed by the blue circle.

The blue area in front of the goal net and goal line is the goal crease. This is designed as a safe area for the goalie, where he cannot legally be hit or knocked down by opposing players.

HOCKEY OFFICIATING

If your home ice is the hosting ground for a tournament, hockey-parent volunteers are expected to divide their time working as minor officials or assisting with registration and other hosting roles. As a hockey mom, you might be called by your division rep or team manager to help out as a minor official—

Mite centers Tyler Creagh, left, and Jimmy Collias, right, face off.   *Photo by Andrew Doig*

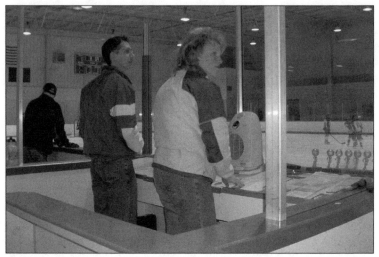

Andy Oliver, Mite Division Rep of the Grand Traverse Hockey Association, and hockey mom Becky Hart work as minor officials at the Grand Traverse Invitational Mite B Tournament in Traverse City, Michigan.

scorekeeper or timer—during a tournament game. You might even fill the role at regular house games.

When a goal is scored or a penalty is called, the referee approaches the minor officials from the referee's crease to give them information about the goal or penalty. The timer will stop the clock and, for a penalty, start the penalty timer. The scorekeeper will record the time and goal, identifying who scored and assisted, or the penalty, identifying the violation type and violating player(s).

Infractions

Also called violations, infractions frequently stop play on the ice. If the officials consist of a referee and two linesmen (some games are officiated by two referees), the job of a linesman is to look for infractions. After a linesman calls an infraction, the game resumes with a face-off. These breaches are not serious enough to warrant a penalty, which would be called by the referee, and which would take

WHERE IT'S PLAYED

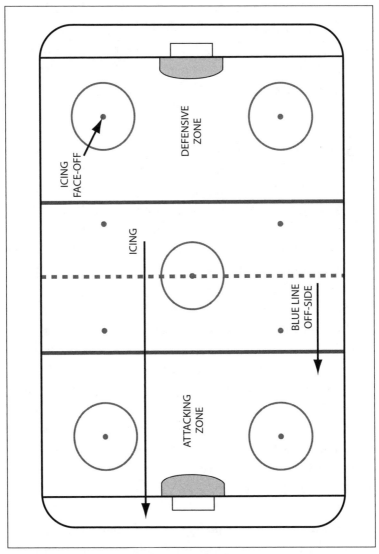

A standard ice hockey rink measures about 185 feet to 20 feet long and 85 feet wide. The ice is replenished with a large machine called a Zamboni, which sprays a new coat of water over the surface. Refrigeration technology beneath the surface quickly freezes the water to create a smooth and solid new layer of ice.

the offending player out of the game for two to ten minutes, or for the remainder of the game for major misconduct offenses. The most frequent infractions are icing—shooting the puck from behind the center line to the opponent's goal line untouched when both teams have an equal number of players on the ice—and the offside—a player moving ahead of the puck in the attacking (offensive) zone.

Penalties

When issuing penalties the referee must not only determine the offense but judge the intent—whether it was accidental, careless, or malicious, meant to injure an opponent. Rookie hockey parents should keep in mind that a referee officiating a Mites game may often choose not to blow the whistle on incidents that are seemingly violations to spectators in the stands. When officiating Mites, the referee will often assume the benefit of unintended collision as Mites are in the early stages of developing their skating (turning and stopping) ability.

The severity in wrongful conduct establishes the degree of penalty, beginning with a minor two-minute penalty to a major five-minute to ten-minute misconduct to getting kicked out of the game. A player may earn a double penalty, such as a double minor—serving two consecutive two-minute periods in the penalty box—for hooking an opponent over and over, for example. Be warned that parents can get thrown out of the rink by refs as easily as players or coaches for arguing or fighting in the stands. Some offenses automatically reap a particular degree of penalty in most instances. They are categorized in the following way:

Minors: two minutes in the penalty box; if the short-handed team is scored against because of the penalty, the player in the box may immediately rejoin his team

Boarding—slamming an opponent into the boards

Charging—checking with excessive speed

Cross-Checking—checking an opponent with the stick across the body

Elbowing—checking an opponent with the elbow extended

High-Sticking—contacting an opponent with the stick higher than the opponent's shoulders; also hitting the puck in the air with the stick higher than shoulder height

Holding—impeding an opponent's progress on the ice by using the hand or stick, commonly holding on to his jersey

Hooking—using the stick to hold back an opponent

Interference—impeding the progress of an opponent who is not in possession of the puck

Roughing—striking another player, but not actually fighting (meaning the gloves haven't dropped off yet)

Slashing—hitting an opponent with the stick to hold him or hurt him

Tripping—obstructing the opponent's leg to cause him to fall

Majors: five minutes in the penalty box; does not terminate early

Butt-Ending—hitting an opponent with the top of the shaft of the stick

Checking from behind—checking an opponent directly from behind, completely out of range of his view so that he cannot brace himself for the check

Fighting—referred to as "fisticuff" in the NHL, dropping the gloves and duking it out on the ice

Spearing—jabbing an opponent with the stick blade

Match penalty: ejection from the game; in addition, another teammate must serve five to ten minutes in the penalty box

Misconducts: usually ten minutes in the penalty box, but a team cannot be short a player for over two to five minutes

Game misconduct—ejection from the game and suspension from the next game

Gross misconduct—ejection from the game and the possibility of ejection from the league upon evaluation of the case by league administrators

ICE HOCKEY OFFICIALS' SIGNS
Courtesy of the NCAA

Boarding
Strike the clenched fist of one hand into the open palm of the other hand directly in front of the chest.

Butt-Ending
A crossing motion of the forearms, one moving under the other.

Charging
Rotating clenched fists around one another in front of chest.

Checking (Relevant to girls'/women's hockey and Mite and Squirt youth levels)
The nonwhistle hand is placed on the shoulder and then moved out and to the side.

Clipping
Keep both skates on the ice when signaling, using right hand on the leg.

Delay of Game
The nonwhistle hand, palm open, is placed across the chest and then fully extended directly in front of the body.

Roughing
Fists clenched, fully extending arm from the side.

Grasping the Face Mask
A single or double motion as if grasping a face mask and pulling it down.

Goal Scored
Point at the net with the nonwhistle hand, palm opened.

Interference
Crossed arms with fists clenched stationary in front of chest.

Holding the Stick
Clasp wrist of whistle hand with the other hand well in front of chest. Next, hold both fists, clenched, one a short space in front of the other at waist height.

Obstruction
Hands in the middle of body in the shape of an "O."

Holding
Clasp wrist of whistle hand with the other hand well in front of the chest.

"Wash-Out"
Both arms swung shoulder height, not waist height.

Icing
The back official signals the icing situation by fully extending the free arm (without whistle) at a 65 degree angle. The front official shall indicate the icing is completed by extending the free arm over the head, up straight, and blowing the whistle. The back official then will move to the face-off spot and cross arms to indicate the icing.

Contact to the Head
Extend arm above head and tap hand with open palm.

Cross-Checking
A signal forward and back motion with both fists clenched in front of the chest.

Hitting from Behind
Arm placed behind the back, elbow bent, forearm parallel to the ice surface.

Fighting/Punching
A double "punching" motion with fists clenched, fully extended in front of the body.

Elbowing
Tapping either elbow with the opposite hand.

Intentional Offside
After blowing whistle for offside, point toward offending team's special spot with nonwhistle hand.

Spearing
A single jabbing motion with both hands together, thrust forward in front of the chest, then dropping hands to the side.

Slashing
One chop with the nonwhistle hand across the straightened forearm of the other hand.

Tripping
Keep both skates on the ice when signaling, using right hand on the leg.

Timeout/Unsportsmanlike Conduct
Using both hands to form a "T" in front of the chest.

Hooking
A series of tugging motions with both arms, as if pulling something toward the stomach.

Kneeing
A single slapping of the right palm to the right knee, keeping both skate blades on the ice.

Penalty Shot
Arms crossed (fists clenched) above the head.

Delayed Offsides
Extend arm in the air and point in line with other arm.

High-Sticking
Holding both fists, clenched, one a short space immediately above the other side of the head.

Delayed Calling of Penalty
Extend arm to upright position.

Hand Pass
The nonwhistle hand (open hand) and arm are placed straight down alongside the body and swung toward and up once in an underhand motion.

Misconduct
Hands should be moved once from sides down to hips. Thus, point to player first, hands to hips second.

HOCKEY SPEAK

You may feel as if the hockey fanatics sitting around you in the stands are speaking a foreign language as they call the play as they see it. It's not French they're speaking; it's hockey speak. Refer to the glossary at the end of this book when translating hockey speak into layman's, or laymom's, language. By next season, you might be interpreting for a fellow rookie hockey mom who's not as up on the lingo as you are.

Hockey-Speak Translated

Don't bunch up.
"Play your positions."

Oh man, the poor kid; he fanned on that one.
"Darn, the child completely missed the puck with the blade of his stick after making a sweeping motion."

She fed it—tape-to-tape.
"She passed the puck well. It was received easily by the intended receiver."

He's in the slot! He's in the slot!
"There's a teammate waiting in front of the goal for a pass. You ought to pass it."

Did you see how the kid deked the goalie to her backhand on that breakaway?
"Did you see how the child skated with the puck, so fast that not one opposing player could defend the goal against her? Then how she made the goalie think that she was going to shoot the puck into the goal with the outer curved part of the blade of her stick instead of the inner part?"

Beauty! Coast to coast, baby!
"Yeah! One of our players carried the puck from the defensive zone, through the neutral zone, into the offensive zone, and to the net."

She put the biscuit in the basket.

"She scored a goal."

We'll have to roof it. The goalie's standing on his head.

Mite forwards drive to the net.
Photo by Andrew Doig

"The player on our team should try to shoot the puck airborne into the net, high enough to reach under the top of it. The goalie is displaying sharp reflexes and skill, making several saves in a row; it's really hard to get a puck by him that's shot low."

What are the line rules at this tournament, buzzer or change on the fly?

"Do the tournament rules mandate that the children play in predetermined forward and defensive lines that change every two minutes, or can the coach spontaneously order line changes during active play?"

Who's the draw man?

"Who is taking the face-off for our team?"

He had a lot of mustard on that shot.

"He shot the puck with great power."

She plays bigger than her size.

"She's playing more intensely than one might assume for her level."

Let's get some D out there.

"Take the puck away from the other team by sweeping your sticks to move the puck out from in front of the player who is now controlling it. Come on defense."

Clear it!

"Come on defense. Get the puck and play away from the front of our team's net."

He put that through the five hole!

"The player successfully shot the puck through the area between the goaltender's pads."

He crashed the net.

"He skated aggressively to the net to receive a pass or pick up a loose puck."

They're looking for the garbage goal.

"The forwards are skating close in front of the offensive goal waiting for a rebound to shoot in."

Who's in the sin bin?

"Which child is sitting in the penalty box?"

The kid got called for chirping to the zebra.

"The child was sent to the penalty box with an unsportsmanlike penalty or misconduct for talking back to the official."

Let's hope you never hear this last one about someone on your team! Also note, that not all of these utterances are exactly positive. Nonetheless, you'll hear them said, Mom. You ought to know what they mean in plain English.

Mite defenseman Jacob Troyer transitions the puck from his defensive zone to the neutral zone while being pursued by opponents.

Photo by Andrew Doig

SOME MORE TERMS DEFINED

Bag skate—skating sprint laps; a coach might call for the bag skate as a discipline tool or as a means of getting out-of-shape skaters into shape

Barn—a hockey arena

Biscuit—the puck

Blueliner—a defenseman

Bulging the twine—scoring a goal

Catlike reflexes—play swiftness, usually referring to the goalie's ability to block the puck with his body or catch the puck in his glove

Cherry-Picking—an offensive player waiting behind the play looking for a breakaway pass

Chiclets—teeth (wearing a mask and mouth guard will prevent your child from "spitting chiclets")

Dangle—(a verb) has to do with savvy stickhandling and puck control

Finisher—the player whom the others frequently pass to for a shot of the puck in net

Goon—a large player who often blocks opponents; in the NHL these are the "enforcers," the guys who are good at annoying opponents

Grinder—a thoroughly aggressive player, who gives 100 percent for his team; if a hockey dad refers to your kid as a "grinder," he is complimenting your kid.

Headman—(a verb) moving the puck up by passing it to a teammate

Lumber—a hockey stick

One-Timer—a swift shot on goal directly off receiving a pass

Screen—blocking the goalie's view to gain a scoring advantage

Shot blocker—a defenseman who not only blocks with his stick but also with his body

Spinorama—a 180-degree spin by the player carrying the puck

Tape-to-tape—a flawless pass

Tic-tac-toe—three rapid, flawless passes

Top end—the best players on a team

Top shelf—the high part of the net; a player may aim for the "top shelf" when shooting on goal

The room—the fraternity and solidarity of the team, the sanctum of the team where what's said stays within the team, "stays in the room"

Traffic—putting a "screen" in front of the opposing goalie

Twig—a hockey stick

4

Equipment Manager Mom

. . . the first pair of skates I got came about as a result of my mother's kindness. Mum had a little cup and she kept whatever change she had in there. And one day some lady came to the door. I think my mother recognized her. This was during the Depression, when there was little or no money and no jobs. My dad did have some jobs, because he could work with his hands and do so many mechanical things. And when this woman came to our door, I believe she was trying to get milk money for her family. My mother gave her some, and the lady gave Mum what she had in a gunnysack. It was like an old potato sack.

My mother came over with the sack, and I remember sitting down and waiting, because we had no idea what was in the sack. She dumped the sack over and, among some other things, there were skates inside.

—Gordie Howe in *And Howe!*

With today's strict safety-driven equipment guidelines in youth hockey, getting the equipment together for an ice hockey player is a major project, especially if you have multiple skaters and you're looking for bargains. First of all, Mom, you must keep in mind a very important rule as you stockpile that equipment: you have to be 100 percent sure that the equipment fits perfectly. Don't think that it's OK to get skates or padding a little on the large side, because "he'll grow into it." Your skater could suffer injuries from equipment that doesn't fit right. Purchase hockey equipment at a hockey equipment store or sporting goods store that has earned a good reputation for fitting hockey players with equipment. Sales people at such stores are trained in helping customers get equipped for hockey, unlike their counterparts at the chain superstores.

A Mini-Mite in equipment, without jersey.

An important point to keep in mind when buying used or discontinued equipment is to be sure that it's regulation, meaning it is approved by the HECC (Hockey Equipment Certification Council). HECC certification is good for five years. For meeting equipment guidelines and for promoting optimal player safety, used equipment must not be out of date or overly used.

Most leagues have goalie pads, chest protector, stick, blocker, and glove available to loan to

Mini-Mite-, Mite-, and Squirt-level goaltenders. Goalie equipment is more costly than position-player equipment. You'll want to be sure your skater is dedicated to playing net before you invest in the equipment.

This Mini-Mite (see photo, p. 56) is equipped with all but his jersey. Not seen is the jock and jock shorts, or strap, which go on first. Next are the shin/knee guards (Velcro straps are fastened to go toward the outside of the calf), then the hockey socks (knit tubes). Put the protective pants on next and fasten the belt snugly or attach suspenders. The skates can go on anytime after the pants. Fit the chest protector/shoulder pads, then the elbow pads (usually labeled "right" or "left"). The jersey would go on next, then the neck guard, helmet, and gloves.

Do not dress your hockey player too warmly underneath the gear. For indoor-rink hockey, dressing him in a thin short- or long-sleeved shirt, normal underwear, and one pair of sports socks is appropriate for how active hockey players get on the ice. They sweat; don't worry about your player getting cold out there.

THE SKATES

Good skates are made of synthetic leather on the interior, called Clarino, that is specially fabricated to be water resistant, durable, and flexible. The exterior of the skates is covered in a nylon material. Plastic runners hold the metal blades.

In most, not all, brands, good-fitting skates are about one shoe size smaller. Bauer® models tend to run narrow, while CCM® models tend to run wider. Skates should fit snugly with only one pair of warm socks. You should be able to fit two fingers behind your child's heel in unlaced skates. If you're still not sure of their fit, simply take the sole pad out of the skate, set it on the floor and have your skater stand on it. This way, you'll get an accurate reading of the skate's width and length in relation to your child's foot.

Your newer, high-performance brands of skates offer a technology called thermoformability. These skates have a gel padding that is heated to form to the skater's foot. After you've paid for the skates, the salesperson will heat the skates; then your child will put the skates on and sit for a while to allow the gel padding to form to the shape of his foot. You need to keep this thermo-fit feature in mind when purchasing used skates at that garage sale or rink equipment exchange. You're not just looking for a bargain on a certain size, but on a special fit for your skater. The previous owner's foot shape will have to match your skater's.

Have your skater walk around in any nonthermoform new skates or used skates you're considering purchasing. In properly laced-up skates, your skater's toes should come to the end of the skate with no wrinkles in the instep and heel padding. She should be able to wiggle her toes. There should be a space of an inch to an inch and a half over the instep of the tightly laced, but not overly tight, skates.

Lacing the skates properly is important for how the skates contribute to your skater's performance on the ice. They must be laced tight enough so that the skate supports the entire foot and ankle well. That means, Mom, that you have to pull them from the bottom of the boot to the top. A hooked tool that'll cost you about two bucks at any gear shop will save your nails and knuckles from wear and tear. Also, an investment in waxed laces makes the task much easier.

Waxed laces will also contribute to ease in delacing—another important ritual to get right for maintaining the skates. You must delace the boot all the way, from top to bottom, so that the skate comes off easily. If you force off a tight skate, a boot that's not delaced enough, you'll destroy the skate's padding.

You can also eliminate some of the struggle from the lacing/delacing routine by preserving your child's laces from fraying. Dip the ends in nail polish for a few seconds and let the polish dry as a shield for the ends of the laces.

Hockey mom Colleen Vogel laces up son Zach's skates before his Mite team's competition.

For optimal skating performance, be sure that your child's skate blades are sharp. You will need to take them to a rink pro shop or sporting goods store to be sharpened about every six to eight weeks during a season. Make sure an expert does the sharpening. Poor sharpening could destroy the blades of those skates you just spent a half-day's pay on. A good test that your skater's blades are adequately sharp will require that you sacrifice a nail. Run the white part of a long fingernail along the blades (keep flesh safely away from the blade). If they can slice a fingernail, they're sharp enough for stellar skating. Make sure to dry the skate blades with a soft cloth soon after your skater is off the ice to prevent the blades from rusting. Also, invest in good-fitting skate guards, plastic or rubber fittings for the blades, so that the blades do not come into contact with wood, cement, metal, or any other material that could damage them. Don't leave the guards on the blades when you pack the skates away in the hockey bag, however. Moisture will creep in between the guards and blades and cause the metal to rust. Store the skates in a cloth bag or loose with a pair of soakers on the blades. Soakers are cloth wraps that you can purchase at any rink pro shop.

Some skaters specify particular sharpening in order to adjust the radius of the blade—to control the amount of the blade that scrapes the ice. The larger the radius the more straightaway speed a skater will have. A forward, valuing the agility of quick and frequent stops and turns, will prefer a smaller radius, while a defenseman will want more blade for good balance as he checks an opponent. Shortening the radius of a blade is called "rocking" the skate. Skates are automatically rocked each time they are sharpened. Therefore, if you have a defenseman, he may need skates on the newer side or replacement blades.

Goaltenders require special skates. Yes, they're more expensive, as you might have guessed. This is because they have a longer blade and the boot has a special "goal shell" covering it.

THE STICK

If your child has never played hockey before, you'll want to buy him a basic youth stick with a straight blade. Do not assume that your child's shooting preference will match the hand he prefers to color with. In other words, your child may color right-handed but become a lefty shooter in hockey. After your Pre-Mite outgrows this first stick and is ready for his next stick, let him pick out his stick at the hockey shop. He'll have developed some preference by then, and it's important that he have a sense of ownership in his stick choice. Novice players quickly establish shooting-direction preference and need a blade curved accordingly. Young players also evolve their stick-holding preference, which might demand a longer or shorter shaft than the conventional to-the-chin-with-skates-on length (explained below).

The most common sticks are the woods, which are actually made with fiberglass. Some sticks have shafts made of aluminum, graphite, or titanium with a wood blade attached. Blades are curved to the left for right-handed shooters and to the right for left-handed shooters. Goalie sticks have a wide section in the middle of the shaft and a straight blade that is longer and wider than a player's stick. Sticks come in three degrees of flex, or stiffness: medium, stiff, and extra stiff. Players who shoot harder need strong flex, while forwards who shoot snap shots closer to the net may want weaker flex, or a less stiff, more flexible stick.

Your child will choose her stick according to proper lie, or the angle between the blade and shaft. A player's lie is determined by whether she carries the puck close to her feet or away. If unsure, it's probably safe to get a stick with a lie of five or six for a very young skater. You also need to choose the correct length, or cut down a stick to the correct length. Convention says that a player's proper stick length is the height of his chin from the ice with his skates on, but your skater might prefer a different length.

You should buy tape for your child's stick. As he gets older he'll develop his own preference for taping his stick. If you're getting your Pre-Mite skater her first stick, you may want to have a friend who plays

The general rule for the length of a youth hockey stick is to the nose with skates off, to the chin with skates on.

hockey or someone at the pro shop assist you in taping the blade and the knob (top) of the shaft to make it easier for your skater to control the puck. Taping the blade cushions the puck and also leaves a mark on the blade that will indicate whether or not the stick has the proper lie for the skater. Taping the knob makes the stick more comfortable to grip and easier to hold on to during active play. It also prevents the stick from cutting into the material of the gloves. Even if you have a Pre-Mite skater, you should get in the practice of taping his stick. He'll like that; little kids love tape.

WHAT IT WILL COST YOU

One season's ice time	$500–$1,000
Camps and clinics	$130–$700 per course
Average tournament cost	$500–$700 per team

EQUIPMENT

The cost range includes youth sizes and the least expensive brands to the most expensive.

Player

Skates	$60–$200
Skate guards	$10
Skate blades	$30
Stick	$15 plus
Helmet without cage	$45–$70
Helmet with cage	$60–$90
Mouth guard	$3–$20
Shoulder pads/chest protector	$20–$100

Throat protection	$5–$15
Elbow pads	$15–$35
Pants—hip and thigh protection	$40–$100
Suspenders (not mandatory)	$10–$20
Shin guards (includes knee protection)	$20–$75
Gloves	$20–$50
Practice jersey	$15–$25
Socks	$10–$15
Jock cup and supporter	$10–$40
Hockey duffle bag	$35–$75

Goalie

Skates	$120 plus
Stick	$30–$80
Mask	$200 plus
Throat protection	$35–$50
Chest/arm pads	$45–$185
Blocker pads	$45–$160
Leg pads	$120–$300
Catching gloves	$80–$150
Goal jock	$35–$50

Count on having to secure new equipment for your child at least once per season. Search garage sales, used-sporting-goods shops, hockey-rink swap sales, and newspaper and Internet classified ads for previously owned equipment. You'll save 50 to 75 percent of what the equipment costs brand new. HECC certification expires in five years; so you want to buy newer used equipment.

Mite Katelyn Tomlian gears up before a game.

PROTECTIVE GEAR
The Helmet

Take your child with you when you choose a helmet and get someone who is experienced in ice hockey to fit it to your child's head. There are two screws on each side of the helmet that work to alter the width. Make sure you have a face-mask fitted for the helmet. Even if your child is only at the Pre-Mite or learn-to-skate level, make him wear facial protection. USA Hockey, which sets the rules and guidelines for youth hockey leagues, requires players to wear a mask. Be careful when purchasing a cage or shield separately from the helmet; not all cages and shields fit all helmets. A properly fitting helmet will fit comfortably to your child yet not move around on his head with the strap untied. The front of the helmet will reach within a finger's width from the child's eyebrows. The chin cup should rest comfortably under the child's chin with his mouth closed. Be sure that your child's ears are well covered. Most helmets come equipped with removable ear guards.

The Pads and Protectors

Your child will also need several pieces of protective gear, including a chest protector with shoulder pads, a neck guard, elbow pads, thigh- and hip-padded pants, shin guards with kneepads, protective cup, and hockey gloves. It is not wise to buy these items on the large side; so you will need to fit your child in new protective equipment each year. Loose padding will leave your child unprotected on the ice and more vulnerable to injury. If your skater is bodychecked or collides into something or someone, ill-fitting pads will jam into her, bruising tissue.

The Cup

Many leagues require players to wear jock cups, even the nonbodychecking little Mites and Squirts, and even the girls. This is probably the piece of equipment you'll feel most ill-qualified to scout out and buy. So buy what I bought. I got my skaters the shorts that have the cup built right in. That way I didn't have to deal with the strap and the cup separately and teach five-year-olds how to put the contraption on. I just handed them the shorts and said, "Put this on over your underwear. Tag goes in back." It was simple.

THE CLOTHING

Until your skater gets used to the elbow pads and shin guards, which usually come with Velcro tabs, her delicate skin may become irritated from the rubbing. You may want to have your skater wear a thin, long-sleeved T-shirt and thin, pajama-like long pants under the equipment until the skin toughens up or until she complains about the geekiness and uncoolness (I mean this both literally and figuratively) of wearing all those clothes.

THE SOCKS

You'll need to equip your skater with hockey socks as well—those goofy, knitted, striped leggings hockey players wear. They look like something Grandma would knit and make a kid wear so he wouldn't catch cold on the ice. Well, some grandmother in Canada is probably behind the first hockey socks, which, since they don't cover the feet, aren't really socks at all; they're long tubes that fit around the leg, over the shin guards and kneepads. Your Mite or Squirt might consider you a cool mom for taping up the socks, which means getting special sock tape (for about a dollar or two a roll) and taping around the ankle and around the knee about two times. Not only will your skater look like a real, big-time player, his leg gear will fit even more securely and comfortably. Then, after the skate, your young skater will have fun making a tape ball with the used tape and shooting it around the locker room with his buddies while you're packing up the bag and chatting with other parents.

THE GLOVES

The gloves are very big and bulky. Have your skater practice wearing them on the iced pond, at your local rink's open skate, or on the in-line skate course that is your driveway or cul-de-sac. The gloves should be broken in, and your skater will need to get the hang of picking up things, like sticks, with them. It requires practice.

WASHING AND DESTINKING THE EQUIPMENT

The ice may appear white, but it sure ain't clean. Just thinking of the spit that accumulates out there alone ought to get you in the habit of washing the jerseys and equipment regularly. I've heard of moms washing helmets by putting them on the top rack of their dishwasher. They say it works. I wash the socks and jerseys in the washing machine with the delicate cycle in cold water. Soaking a light-colored jersey marked with board stains and dirt in the washing machine with some dishwasher powder before throwing it in the regular wash will destain it and brighten it up. To clean and destink the chest protector and padded pants, set them in a bathtub filled with cold water and laundry soap. Soak for about an hour, rinse, and set in the sun to dry. When removing the equipment, you'll feel satisfied that you succeeded in achieving cleanliness when you see how dirty the water is.

Despite what you may have heard at the rink, your minivan or Suburban need not necessarily permanently carry the odor of a hockey locker room. Those hockey bags need not infect that important trunk space, where you also haul groceries, with stink germs. And you need not attach a hockey mom bumper sticker to the exterior of your vehicle to explain the rink odor that follows you out of the car.

Mom, it's definitely worth the little time and effort that's required to air out your skater's equipment after every practice and game. There's a lot of hard play and sweating out on the ice. If you keep the equipment stored away tightly in a duffle bag, it'll get full of mold and fungus and grow very stinky quickly. Open up that bag when your child gets home from the rink and air out all the equipment on a blanket on your back lawn or on a drying line in your basement. For more peace of mind (and peace of nose), you can toss a car air freshener in the bag or insert the cardboard air fresheners in your child's gloves and skates, but make sure your child approves of the scent. You wouldn't want to embarrass your skater by making his equipment smell perfumey and pretty.

If the equipment still stinks to high heaven despite your best efforts, you can have it professionally destinked. There are special cleaning services that will kill the bacteria, mold, and odor populating your skater's equipment, so that it will no longer be located by scent before sight.

5

Agent Mom

In 1972 very few mothers encouraged their daughters to
participate in any type of sport, especially one as rough as
hockey. And even though the idea certainly was not her
own, my mother not only allowed me to play, she encouraged me every step of the way. From the time I was ten
years old to the day I entered college, she made me feel
that my hockey "career" was as important as my brother's.
When others looked at me and said, "YOU play hockey?"
(a phrase I still hear today), she was the first to respond,
"She certainly does!"

—Jody Bruce, defenseman for the Remax Stars
in the Advanced "A" Division of the Metro Skaters
Hockey League (MSHL) in Michigan and former
player at Colby College (early 1980s)

What do I mean by "agent mom?" You're not really a sports
agent, charging fees to land a player on a team. What
you are for your youth hockey player is her advocate, a
representative on her behalf. If playing hockey means a lot to your

child (forget what it means to you), then your job, Mom, is to find the right fit for her. You begin by scouting out the best league— small, medium, large—for your player. Then you do your best to see that she is drafted by a good coach.

A GOOD COACH

By "a good coach," in reference to early-level youth hockey, I don't necessarily mean the winningest coach. A good coach, especially of very young players, will clearly work to develop every player on the team. Player development will take precedence to team standings; a coach who develops each player will likely see his team evolve into a group of kids who will learn to perform well as part of the single unit of a team. In the long run, the players' sense of team is critical for hockey success, which is all about having fun and learning the game. In other words, a Mites coach, for example, who will not give ice time to both the more developed and less developed players is a coach who lacks an understanding of the primary goal of early-level youth hockey, which is to develop all the players and to turn them into individuals who practice the discipline of playing for the team. A good coach delicately balances the individual development of players with what's good for the team.

It is likely that the greatest adult influence on your young hockey player besides you and Dad is the hockey coach. Not only will the coach teach the nuts and bolts, Xs and Os, and skills and drills of hockey, he will become a significant model to your child of self-control, patience, a responsible work ethic, and sportsmanship. Your child's coach will for better or worse affect his self-esteem and sense of respect toward others. If you're a single mom and your child's father is not a strong influence in his life, the hockey coach might be his most dominate adult-male influence. Choose your coach wisely, and make him accountable for the development of his players. Of course, don't neglect to show your gratitude to the coach for his commitment of time, energy, and emotions. Like, motherhood, coaching can be a daunting and thankless effort.

At the rink, hockey moms can benefit from practicing the art of diplomacy. Before fueling criticism of your child's coach, talk to him when you're calm, opening the conversation with, "Is there anything I can do to help my child's hockey development?" This is a positive way to launch a constructive parent-to-coach conversation, during which you'll have an opportunity to express your concerns politely.

If your player happens to fall under the direction of a clearly unreasonable coach, follow up with your concerns according to your hockey association's grievance policy. You should not be forced to tolerate a coach who does not conduct himself in a manner fitting of a child's major adult influence. Your standards for a coach's character must be high. If a reasonable discussion with the coach or division representative does not resolve the problem and if the situation is truly damaging to youth players, you may decide to write a letter to the league board.

THE LEAGUES OUT THERE

To get information about hockey leagues, clubs, and camps, you can simply call your local rinks or contact your state's or province's youth hockey association. You'll also find it very easy to search resources on the Internet for youth hockey opportunities in your area.

Not only can you find youth hockey programs for able-bodied children, you can also find programs for disabled children. Sled Hockey is for the disabled youth athlete who cannot stand or walk. Special Hockey is for youth athletes who are developmentally disabled. Amputee Hockey is for youth athletes who are missing one or more limbs. There are also programs known as Hockey for the Blind and Hearing Impaired Hockey. Visit www.usahockey.com for more information about youth hockey programs for disabled children.

You will enroll beginner skaters in an instructional program. If your child is age seven and has developed some hockey skating and stickhandling skills, you can enroll him in a "house" recreational league as a Mite. Question your child's Pre-Mite skating or hockey instructor to assess thoroughly and carefully your child's abilities and interests in the sport. You also ought to realistically consider what you can invest financially and timewise. If your child really loves the sport but you worry about the money and time you have available to you, you might want to recruit financial and shuttling assistance from close relatives, perhaps as a birthday or holiday gift to your child. You can also organize a carpooling arrangement with other hockey parents to free up some time for your many other responsibilities as a parent.

The cornerstone of a hockey association's ability to offer healthy leagues is its Pre-Mite hockey program. Typically, if the learn-to-skate and Tyke/Mini-Mites programs are well run and growing, the association's leagues are well run and growing, too. The association prioritizes hockey development, the parents know each other and care about the well-being of all the kids, the kids have bonded with one another, and the bar for developmental standards and instructional excellence is set high.

I cannot stress enough how important it is to investigate your local hockey associations to find a league that would best suit your child's hockey development needs. Don't just sign her up at the rink closest to your home. Perhaps the rink ten minutes farther would be a better choice. Evaluate carefully what kind of skater and player your child really is. Talk to professional instructors to assess the best program match for your child.

You'll find that there is a significant difference among hockey associations when it comes to resources available for the development of the youngest, Pre-Mite hockey and hockey divisions offered for girl players. There is also a difference in the degree of priority placed on winning. Ask around, and you may discover a more relaxed attitude among hockey parents in one hockey association, while another hockey association tends to attract parents who are more "hockey crazy," if you will. The latter may have house players that are more developed in skills, but that is no guarantee; it may be that these house players have a reputation of playing a more physical, gritty game (to put it kindly). Ask around about the reputations of different leagues in your area. Competition to make a Tier-II travel team (see the "Travel Teams" section later in this chapter) also varies among associations, as does the performance among players in its house divisions. A kid who didn't make the travel, or rep, team of one association and is forced to play house, might be a shoo-in on the travel team of another hockey association.

When doing your homework to find a healthy league for your child, keep in mind that youth hockey players thrive in an environment that challenges them appropriately. They should sense they're improving while being driven to continue improving. Do the research, ask around, and then go with your gut. Trying out different novice programs, like a Mini-Mites program, one season at one rink and the next at another is a good way to investigate league opportunities for your future Mite. Increasingly more rinks are offering young skater recruitment events. Attend these as well. Then talk with your child about where she had the most fun. You and your player can then make a decision together on where to begin participating in Mite-level team playing.

GIRLS' HOCKEY

Though USA Hockey included in its guidelines classifications for Girls 10 and Under (10U) and Girls 8 and Under (8U) (as of June 2004), many hockey leagues mix the genders in their Mites (eight and under) and Squirts (ten and under) divisions. An association's ability to offer 10U and 8U divisions within a girls' league depends on its resources and rate of participation. Because strength and size are equal across gender among young children, there is no physical reason why girls and boys, Squirt and under, cannot play together. At the PeeWee level, however, boys begin bodychecking, unless their team is part of a nonchecking league. Girls' hockey never allows bodychecking at any level.

In the 1970s, when hockey was beginning to be recognized as a sport also for girls, if a league included hockey for girls older than ten, it was one seventeen-and-under rep team. Today, girls above the Squirt level are divided into the divisions of twelve and under (12U), fourteen and under (14U), sixteen and under (16U), and nineteen and under (19U), and it is more common for girls to "play up"— younger players playing out of their age division—than it is for boys. Many U.S. hockey associations still do not have house leagues for girls, rather only rep, or travel, teams. Whether there is a team for each division depends on coaching volunteers and player interest. There is no tier distinction for girls travel hockey at the level of national competition.

HOCKEY SENSE

You'll hear someone comment about a certain player, "The kid's got hockey sense." The comment is not about the kid's skills in skating,

Squirt Jennifer Cusmano shows determination at a tournament in Saginaw, Michigan.

shooting, or stickhandling. Rather it's directed to the *je ne sais quoi* of hockey. Hockey sense is on-ice offensive and defensive awareness and playmaking vision. It's the mysterious sixth sense of the hockey world. It's something that can't be taught, but can be developed if the player is born with the hockey-sense seed. Mom, try as you might, neither you nor the coach can plant that seed, you can only water and feed it if it's there. Hockey sense cannot be forced, only encouraged. It's like a child who can draw well. He is able to observe the world around him, develop a vision of how to express his observations concretely, and then somehow knows how to work his arm, wrist, and fingers to set his vision onto a medium. No one taught him the sense of how to do this. No one can force him to do it. It's the same with hockey sense. It's either there or it's not. Some players are phenomenal skaters with well-honed stickhandling skills, but they don't have hockey sense. A player who is in tune with who's on the ice and where, who can predict where the puck will go, who can pass behind him as if he has eyes in the back of his head, who can spearhead amazing playmaking efforts and penalty killing—this is a player with hockey sense.

THE YOUTH HOCKEY JOURNEY

Veteran hockey moms I've spoken with have all explained to me that parents cannot determine which of today's early-level players will develop into the stars of tomorrow. In other words, though your Mite is one of the lesser performers in skating and stickhandling, this is no indicator of whether or not he'll develop into a high-performing player as a PeeWee or Bantam. A good coach will see past skills to sense and attitude in a young player. Hockey sense can be hidden in young players, still yet unexposed because of underdeveloped skating and stickhandling ability, and good attitude will contribute a great deal to a player's development as he hones his skills. Conversely the six-year-old who can back crossover and has already developed a handy, controlled flip shot, might not evolve into the superstar as some might assume; he may never display any real hockey sense or even any sense of team play and vision. So begin your youth hockey journey recognizing that there is no crystal ball to predict who will shine in the long run and who will drop out of hockey within a few years.

Veteran moms also stress that the number one benefit their own children gained by playing youth hockey was the mark it made on their character. They don't place the value of youth hockey in whether or not a child went on to play college or pro hockey. They tell me that youth hockey helped them parent their child better by enforcing important qualities, like discipline, respect for authority and teammates, self-control, drive, and (believe it or not in light of hockey's reputation for roughness) a highly developed sense of courtesy and politeness. The primary value of youth hockey is not landing your child in the NHL one day or setting him up to earn a college athletic scholarship, it's a venue for training and building his character.

THE LEVELS OF THE JOURNEY

Hockey season begins in early September and lasts until early March, with playoff games in late March and April. Spring hockey leagues play from mid-April through May. Travel hockey is typically a year-round commitment, while house skaters and their parents can relax or get involved in other sports during the off-season. USA Hockey-sanctioned Mini-Mites through Squirts are non-bodychecking levels, and they play with the lighter-weight, bouncy blue puck.

In the United States and Canada a player's play level, or division, is determined by his birth year, though some rep players play up in level. This classification by birth year is why you've probably overheard a hockey mom say something like, "I have a '90 and '92." She is not referring to the model years of the vehicles she drives.

Tiny Skaters

Many rinks offer skating instruction for toddlers that may, by the final level, involve learning to move around the ice in full hockey gear and batting a blue puck around. Instructional skating for tots is often run as part of a rink's or association's learn-to-skate program, which will include children as old as seven and as young as two and a half. Learn-to-skate programs are for the most novice skaters. They are broken down into three or four levels. By the time a child reaches the last level, he or she is ready to move on to either some sort of Pre-Mite hockey instruction or a figure-skating program.

YOUTH HOCKEY DIVISIONS (LEVELS)

Level	Age
Initiation, Beginner, Tiny Tot	2½ and over
Mini-Mite or Pre-Tyke	6 and under
Tyke or Novice	7 and under
Mite	8 and under
Squirt or Atom	10 and under
*PeeWee	12 and under
*Bantam	14 and under
*Midget (Minor)	16 and under
*Midget (Major)	18 and under
*Junior	20 and under
	(see "Juniors" section)

* Girl players participate in girls' divisions identified by age-bracket terminology, rather than the traditional nomenclature for post-Squirt boys. For instance, a thirteen-year-old girl will play 14U (fourteen and under), rather than Bantam. The final level in girls' youth hockey is 19U.

Mini-Mites playing the tag game.

Mini-Mites instructor, Matt Romaniski, teaches a group of six-year-old Mini-Mites (above), who are about to play the tag game, Whales and Sharks. Games are a wonderful means of helping Mini-Mites develop skating agility and speed. As the "whales" skate through the neutral zone, the "sharks" attempt to tag them before they reach the blue line. Other games are Hockey Dodge Ball, Slalom relays, Follow the Leader, or a cone-tipping game called Builders and Destroyers.

Mini-Mites

If your player is five or six, she's just starting. You'll sign her up for a Mini-Mite program. Naturally, she will not yet really know if hockey is the sport she'll continue playing into adulthood. It's normal at this age for kids to bounce from sport to sport. Don't be surprised if suddenly your Mini-Mite decides, midseason, that she wants to quit hockey, even though she was eager to play in the fall. You might ask her why. She'll probably say, "It's not fun." You might want to find out why it's not fun. It could be that someone was mean or that on that particular day she was not feeling well and hockey will be fun again next week. There might not be any reason. Maybe she just doesn't want to get all that equipment on and go out on that cold ice to skate as hard as she can while controlling a bouncy puck. Some parents may force her to stick it through the season. The ice bill is paid by midseason typically. Other parents may take the loss and let their child stay out. At this age, I think your choice must be considered with the child's personality and tendencies in mind. Whatever you decide, Mom, don't call your Mini-Mite a quitter or a baby for wanting to drop hockey. Stop for a moment and think hard about how very young she still is. While hockey is fun for many, it's tedious and difficult for others. Personally, I've found that many Mini-Mites who sit it out for a while return to the rink later that season or start skating again as Mites (the next age level up). I believe the child must feel she has ownership of her hockey decision.

Mini-Mites is youth hockey's most developmental and noncompetitive level. It's the next step up in skating from a tot's learn-to-skate program. It's the level that parents decide to invest in hockey skates as opposed to figure skates. Typically, Mini-Mites meet two times a week for an hour session. The kids develop forward and crossover skating, skating backward, stopping, stickhandling, and basic puck control and shooting techniques. They may play a half-hour, cross-ice or full-ice scrimmage once a week or so. Instructors do not yet enforce the rules of offsides and icing. They just let the little ones go at it and get the feel of carrying a puck in active play. A few volunteer Mini-Mites will step into the net to see if goaltending is their cup of tea. If your Mini-Mite is one of those special kids with dreams of playing net, don't worry about running out and buying goalie gear. Your Mini-Mites director should have a couple sets of goaltending pads, blockers, and gloves to be shared by those interested in trying out the net.

Mite Howard DeHooghe makes a chest save. The goaltender is an extremely dedicated athlete. Like many youth-hockey goalies, Howard develops his skill through lessons with a private goalie coach, as well as participating in all of his team's games and practices.

Photo submitted by Peter and Linda DeHooghe

Mites

Mites is the level at which tracked team competition begins. Though the games count now, meaning that individual stats and team standings are kept by the league, parents must keep in mind that the games shouldn't matter all that much. Essentially the Mites level is still strongly developmental, or at least ought to be according to the guidelines set by USA Hockey and Hockey Canada.

Ideally, Mite players are aware of offsides and icing rules. They understand that they are not allowed to bodycheck and are developing an awareness of the difference between body contact and bodychecking. They work to avoid infractions and penalties like holding, high-sticking, and tripping. They are discouraged from expressing their frustration by slamming a stick or whining to an official, coach, or other players.

Coaches should be developing Mites in passing and receiving the puck, dribbling the puck, and attacking the net both forehand and backhand. Mites should be strong in their forward start, stride, and stop. Though they are expected to have a limited command of skating backward, the ability to perform backward crossovers is not yet required.

Offensively, they make eye contact with teammates to indicate when they are about to pass or open to receive. Defensively, they understand the importance of maintaining play in zone and how to defend carefully with the stick with a poke check, hook check, or lift-the-stick check. A Mite goalie has skills in stance, shuffling, and gliding. He can move forward and backward and perform stick, body, and glove saves.

Mite players understand the concept of playing zones. The forwards focus on offensive play from all three zones and the defensemen focus on sweeping the puck away from the net and out of the defensive zone into neutral territory where the forwards can carry it into the offensive zone. Mites routinely stretch before a practice or game and understand why playing heads-up hockey is crucial.

Ideally, Mite coaches stress to players that making mistakes is part of developing the skills of the game. They make each player feel that he is a vital member of the team. They emphasize respect for others and abiding by the rules. They require players to commit to the team and to exhibit self-control and discipline, even, and especially, in the face of losing a competition.

Mite players are mainly seven- and eight-year-olds that can barely lace up their own skates. They're little kids. Winning should not be what's stressed at this level. Mite coaches should be expected to allot players equal ice time because the players are still early in their hockey development. According to USA Hockey, in any well-formed Mites division, no team loses more than 30 percent of games and no team wins more than 70 percent. If a Mite team is always winning or always losing, this could be a sign that developmental hockey is not being adequately stressed by the coach or that the league needs to revise its player draft and playtime guidelines. Because USA hockey defines Mites as an early developmental level, the organization, before the 2002–03 season, decided no longer to endorse Mite travel teams. Most state hockey associations followed suit and dropped Mites travel hockey. Nonetheless, parents and league administrators continued to advocate for the reestablishment of Mite travel teams. Even if you're in a league run by a state body that has banned Mite travel teams, you might run across such teams at a rink or tournament near you. After 2003, several organizations supporting Mites travel developed outside USA Hockey recommendations.

Squirts

Squirts build on what they learned as Mites. They develop a knowledge about face-off rules and an awareness of how penalties can arise in the heat of rougher play, such as checking from behind, cross-checking, charging, elbowing, falling on the puck, and interference. You will see more penalty shots at the Squirt level. Squirts are expected to gain greater control in their skating. Skills

Many Mini-Mite programs in rinks around North America are supported by Tim Horton's Restaurants. Your Mini-Mite might sport a Tim Horton's Tim Bits jersey. Look inside the jersey's bottom front. It reads: "I just played hockey. I'm thirsty." After a skate, pop into your local Tim Horton's and have your Mini-Mite show her jersey to a Tim Horton's clerk; she'll receive a complimentary milk or juice and Tim Bits doughnut holes.

in skating will include the backward crossover and stop, one-foot stop, control turn, and lateral motion. In puck control, they will learn to master more complicated dribbling and shifting techniques, puck protection, and give-and-take. They will practice flip passing and receiving with the stick or skate, as well as using board deflection in passing to a teammate. Though bodychecking remains illegal, Squirts focus on body positioning and angling in defending their zone. A Squirt goalie will practice the V-drop and directing rebounds to his teammates. Forwards will practice one-on-one drives and how to play the face-off. They will learn basic offensive strategy, such as the box offense and positioning on entering the offensive zone. Squirt defensemen will begin to depend on one- and two-man forechecking and back-checking techniques in covering the defensive zone. For fitness, Squirts coaches encourage on-ice and off-ice eye-hand coordination activities, as well as more vigorous off-ice conditioning, such as jumping rope and exercise that promotes improved balance and agility. The coach stresses the importance of positive comments among teammates to boost the sense of camaraderie and morale on the team. Squirts are expected to carry their own equipment bag and to dress themselves, as well as to be ready on time for practice or a game. They are practicing juggling schoolwork with hockey.

PeeWees

PeeWees are fine-tuning the speed and exactness of their skating and stickhandling. Passing and receiving are vital to the competitive success of a PeeWee team. Ideally, puck-hogging is no longer tolerated. A PeeWees coach will instruct his team in more sophisticated techniques, such as the wraparound and saucer pass. You will see more breakout play and sophisticated passing at games. PeeWee forwards will try out new moves, like the fake shot, and become much more skilled at taking advantage of rebounds and tipping. PeeWee all-male leagues allow bodychecking (girls' leagues do not introduce bodychecking at any level), so forwards will also have to gain a command of skating through checks safely. Forwards will also have learned specific tactics to take advantage of power-play situations. PeeWee defensemen are developing skills in shot blocking and strategies in defending the net in man-short situations. They understand center-on-point and wings-on-point defensive coverage. The goalie is comfortable and confident in the net. He can now play the puck to his defenseman.

PeeWee off-ice fitness drills might include whiffle-ball stickhandling and other coordination activities. Endurance training could include running the bleachers. Relays and obstacle course workouts will be more common at practice, as well as sprinting and other drills to improve down-ice speed. PeeWees will be more responsible for promoting their own safety. They will know how to treat their injuries with RICE—rest, ice, compression, elevation. PeeWee coaches will depend more on visualization skills among players, namely, picturing plays in their minds. PeeWees are extremely busy managing schoolwork with hockey, and are expected to keep their grades up.

Bantams

Bantams dramatically develop in swiftness and power. This brings the level of game intensity up quite a bit, and it's much harder work for Bantams to maintain control and avoid penalties like slashing and boarding. Because adrenaline kicks in with this level of intensity, the coach may frequently warn against unsportsmanlike conduct. Bantams further develop the more sophisticated skills they worked on as PeeWees, but now skating and passing are quicker and shooting and bodychecking are harder. A Bantam coach will introduce new configurations and positioning and play strategies to his team. Bantams will hone in on the key principles of pressure, transition, support, and control. Forwards will apply triangulation and cycling as a means of getting a puck in net, while defensemen fine-tune their neutral- and defensive-zone coverage strategies.

Ideally, a Bantam coach has a pregame routine in place for his team. Because games are so intense now, the coach has also gone over relaxation and breathing techniques to help players through tense game situations. Bantam coaches must also address the topic of adversity and offer his players strategies in how to cope with and overcome adversity.

Bantams are middle school age—still children, yet often expected to conduct themselves as if they were adults. Often their mind-set has not yet caught up with their size. Fortunately, playing hockey has taught them self-control in the face of adversity and coping skills in the face of peer pressure. Hockey and school demand a lot from them. A Bantam must learn the lesson of how to say no to activities he cannot realistically dedicate himself to. As all but academics is negotiable, he must understand that saying yes to hockey means saying no to many activities other kids his age regularly participate in.

Midgets

Midgets are a condensed group of hockey talent. By this age, those who lacked enough talent or interest in the game have dropped out. At this level, a hockey player must be wholly dedicated to the game and his team. Midgets are expected to develop themselves independently from team practice. What the coach commands them to do at practice is only part of what's expected from them. They must be self-disciplined and dedicated in developing their game and increasing their muscle strength. Midgets must keep hockey in mind when making decisions about what to eat. For example, on game day, four or five small meals are recommended rather than three large meals. A meal should not be consumed less than two hours before a game. Off-season, Midgets continue actively to prepare their bodies for the next season with weight training and aerobic exercise. They will participate in recreational hockey to keep their skills up.

Ideally, a Midgets coach will promote confidence among players. He will require them to travel to games in dress clothes, to carry themselves well, and to exhibit control over their emotions. He will expect 100 percent dedication to the team among players and offer individuals encouragement during times of setback, such as injury or a performance dry spell. A Midgets coach can also expect his players to commit themselves to volunteering activities, including assisting younger league players. Because Midget players are at an age where they can look back and recognize what they have personally gained from hockey, they probably will not challenge a coach's requirement to give back to the sport.

Sources: USA Hockey's *Hockey Education Adult Resource (H.E.A.R.)* manual and its publication for coaches, *Skill Progressions for Player and Coach Development*

Juniors

When your player advances into his late teens, he will have a sense of whether or not highly competitive ice hockey is a sport for him to pursue as an adult. Scouts and coaches from college, juniors, or pros might have already approached him, letting him know they're observing him. Your child may decide to hone his skills and talent in a junior hockey league with the prospect of playing collegiate or professional hockey later.

In its *Official Rules*, USA Hockey describes junior hockey as "the pinnacle of the skill development program of USA Hockey." Junior players are twenty-and-under males who plan to advance their youth hockey development for possible future collegiate or professional opportunities. Junior hockey leagues are structured according to seven guiding principles:

1. To offer players opportunity for skill development
2. To provide players with substantial training and quality coaching
3. To support players' social development and maturity
4. To assist players with educational pursuits
5. To expose players to collegiate and professional scouts and recruiters
6. To enter players into advanced national and international competition
7. To protect players' status as amateurs

JUNIOR LEAGUES

According to USA Hockey's *H.E.A.R.* manual, Tier I and Tier II A junior programs "operate as 'fan-driven' programs," recruiting players nationally and supporting players' tuition, while Tier II B and C programs are locally supported and require players to pay a tuition to finance the team.

U.S. Tier I
United States Hockey League

U.S. Junior A
North American Hockey League

U.S. Junior B
Central States Hockey League
Empire Junior Hockey League
Interstate Junior Hockey League
Metropolitan Junior Hockey League

Minnesota Junior Hockey League
Northern Pacific Junior Hockey League
Western States Hockey League

U.S. Junior C
Continental Hockey Association
Mid-Atlantic Developmental Junior Hockey League

U.S. Independent
Atlantic Junior Hockey League
Continental Elite Hockey League
Eastern Junior Hockey League

Canada Major Junior
Ontario Hockey League
Quebec Major Junior Hockey League
Western Hockey League

Canada Junior A
Alberta Junior Hockey League
British Columbia Junior Hockey League
Canadian Junior Hockey League
Central Junior Hockey League
Manitoba Junior Hockey League
Maritime Junior Hockey League
Northern Ontario Junior Hockey League
Ontario Provincial Junior Hockey League
Quebec Junior AAA Hockey League
Saskatchewan Junior Hockey League
Superior International Junior Hockey League

Canada Junior B
Capital Junior Hockey League
Eastern Ontario Junior Hockey League
Empire Junior Hockey League
Golden Horseshoe Junior Hockey League
Heritage Junior Hockey League
Kootenay International Junior Hockey League
Mid-Western Ontario Junior Hockey League
North Saskatchewan Junior Hockey League
Northwest Junior Hockey League
Pacific International Junior Hockey League
South Saskatchewan Junior Hockey League
Vancouver Island Junior Hockey League
Western Junior Hockey League

Canada Junior C
Empire Junior Hockey League
Central Ontario Junior Hockey League
Georgian Mid-Ontario Junior Hockey League
Great Lakes Junior Hockey League
Niagara Junior Hockey League
Western Ontario Junior Hockey League

WHEN SCOUTS START DROPPING BY

There are different levels of scouting. Initially, scouts maintain a player database with information that traveling scouts have jotted down while at Midget- and Junior-level games. A player may not even know that he's been noticed by a scout and has his name in a database of promising players to be tracked until he becomes eligible for a draft. Each prospect's strengths and weaknesses are evaluated and noted. The scout rates a prospect in the categories of skating, stickhandling, shooting, competitiveness, and hockey sense. The last two categories reveal that scouting is not an entirely objective task; rather it's part scientific and stats-based and part instinct and feeling-based.

If a player gets noticed beyond this preliminary database level, he will likely be approached by a league scout, who will ask him questions and request information about his medical background.

The last level of scouting comes directly from a team's player-personnel department. This scout works closely with a team's general manager or assistant general manager and already knows a great deal about a player before he begins watching him for himself. Nevertheless, he might watch him play over a period of several games before making a decision on recruiting him or not.

TRAVEL TEAMS

Say your child develops into a strong player early on. Some people at the rink have asked you if he's "going out for travel." You need to determine whether it would be best to enroll your child in the recreational house league you've grown accustomed to or give him the option to try out for a competitive travel (rep) team. While house leagues will play most games at the same arena or arenas in one geographic area, and competition is viewed as a means of promoting the tandem ends of fun and skills development, travel teams are purposed to represent the community-based league's or club's top-end talent and are organized for the end of defeating the representative talent of other community-based leagues or clubs.

Travel teams come in three categories. For each division there is single A: first-year players, or players who should be in a lower division because of their age, but are "playing up" as a result of demonstrating remarkable hockey talent and grinder instinct. (House leagues have rules restricting "playing up" the divisions.) Then there is double A for the second-year players. Single A and double A travel teams are known as Tier II travel and represent community-based leagues. Triple-A travel teams play in "elite" Tier I leagues, which are broken down into birth-year-based classifications. Triple-A teams travel a great deal because they compete in leagues encompassing an entire region. For example, in my home state of Michigan, there are only five Triple-A youth clubs; they compete in the Midwest Elite Hockey League. Players frequently travel, often by plane, out of state. Imagine the financial and time commitment they and their parents undertake.

If your child has strong talent and is serious about the sport, you should consider letting him try out for a travel team. Because playing travel will require a great deal of dedication from both you and your child, you will have to make the decision jointly, carefully considering travel hockey's benefits and drawbacks. Travel hockey is expensive and time consuming as teams are required to travel out of town and even out of state frequently during the season. There are relatively few travel opportunities offered to kids under age ten (Squirt/Atom), for good reason. The stress of frequent and out-of-town games and pressure to perform well is too great for many young skaters. Keep in mind that just because your child is selected for a travel team that doesn't guarantee him a superior coach or adequate playing time. Probe the option very carefully.

In "Playing on a Travel Team Is No Vacation," *Good Sports* author Rick Wolff offers straightforward information about the nuances of having a child play travel sports. While playing for the fun of the game lays the foundation for a good house-league experience, travel hockey teams are intended to play to win. Having fun in the pursuit of hockey development is not enough. Travel coaches, therefore, handle their teams from a different perspective than house coaches. Equal playing time, for instance, is not a guiding principle for player development.

You cannot assume that just because your child makes the cut for a travel team that he will improve his skills more than he would on a house team. You cannot assume that he will be better coached and instructed. In fact, the experience may be disappointing for your player. Wolff explained, "Ninety percent of kids polled said they would prefer to play on a losing team than sit on the bench for a winning team." Discuss this reality with your child before he goes out for travel. Wolff maintains that, "The younger the child, the more wary a parent should be." The younger the child—a Squirt or a Mite—the more he is still developing his feelings toward the sport while he increases his hockey knowledge, skills, and sense.

Yet playing on a healthy travel team might be an ideal experience for your child. Even if your child loses game ice time in travel hockey, he may benefit developmentally from the rigorous, skills-building practices he participates in as a member of a travel team. What's more, the sense of camaraderie among travel teammates built from facing the challenge of playing teams from other communities and geographic regions might work to expand your child's character in a positive way, so much so that you recognize travel hockey as becoming a partner in parenting, complementing the values you're working to instill in your child.

Since you are your child's advocate and protector, you will need to anticipate how playing travel could affect him. Before giving your OK for tryouts, know the answers to these questions:

1. What are the travel coach's ethics and priorities?
2. How is the team selected? What are the evaluation categories? For example, is positive attitude considered and sought after?

3. Did last season's travel players and parents have a good experience?

4. How much will it cost in time and money?

5. Does your child understand what travel is about, that he will have to dedicate more time to hockey, perhaps without as much playing time as he would have had on a house team? Is it worth it to him?

6. How healthy are your league's house divisions in promoting development and fun?

7. For furthering his development, will your child be adequately challenged in the house division?

A HEALTHY TEAM

The sign of a healthy team is one with a sense of inclusiveness among players. Each player is greeted by teammates as he enters the locker room. No player is heckled or snubbed by his teammates. There are no cliques, no favored players. Each player is improving and expanding his hockey knowledge and skills. Good players on a healthy team smile at one another. They share games of bubble hockey in a rink lobby after a game. They congratulate a teammate's performance or improvement with a tap and "Good job, buddy." A healthy team has a coach who cares about the development of each player, shows kindness to each, and maintains discipline among all players. A healthy team never jeers opposing players or its own. A healthy team is out to win, of course, but doesn't allow winning to dictate whether the team members are growing as hockey players or having fun learning about the game and about their teammates. Very importantly, the players of a healthy team have parents who exhibit excellence in heads-up parenting. These parents are patient and positive and are very good sports.

TEAM TRYOUTS

Wayne Gretzky earned the moniker "The Great One" because he displayed superiority in the three major categories hockey coaches and judges evaluate: skating, stickhandling, and hockey sense. Seldom will a player shine distinctively in all three categories. Tryout evaluators will look for other qualities as well that make a good hockey player, such as puck aggressiveness, self-control, and an all-around positive attitude.

Unfortunately, players may show up at tryouts thinking they're already a shoo-in because a coach promised them a spot or implied a promise. Your job, Mom, is to keep your player in touch with reality. Delicately explain that this is an unfortunate nuance of real life—that sometimes people make promises they can't keep. Without making him unduly nervous for the tryouts, tell him to show the best that he's got and not to count his chickens too soon. Your player can control only three things when he's on the ice trying out: his preparation, his attitude, and his exhibition of his work ethic and dedication. If he tackles these areas, any insightful and smart coach will take notice of him.

TRYOUT TIPS TO PASS ON TO YOUR PLAYER

- Be sure to stay in shape during the off-season. Grab the in-line skates for some roller hockey over the summer. Soccer, swimming, and bike riding are good for maintaining endurance.
- Do not make tryouts your first time on the ice since last season. Go to open skates at your local rink. Some rinks have a pucks and sticks open skate for hockey players who want to stay in shape.

- Be hungry at tryouts and focused on playing your game. Forget that you're being evaluated, while paying close attention to coach commands. Show enthusiasm for the game.
- Keep in mind that mistakes are common in ice hockey. Missing one pass shouldn't kill your chances in making the team.

THE EXTRAS—SCHOOLS AND CAMPS

There are many hockey camps and schools in the United States and Canada. Chances are you can find one close to your home for your player to attend during summer vacation or winter breaks. Many camps promote fun for the whole family, and you might consider making the spot a destination for a family vacation. While your young hockey player is making new friends and developing his hockey skills, you and the rest of your family can enjoy other facilities that are offered at several hockey camps, including tennis courts and a swimming pool. Some camps are near lakes and beaches or water parks.

Players attend hockey schools and camps for different reasons. Many are simply driven players dedicated to sharpening their skills as much as they can. Developing alongside kids from different geographic regions and associations is a positive experience for them in helping them witness firsthand how players play from other towns and states. Some players attend hockey schools and camps because they're lagging in their development, perhaps because of coming into the sport at a later age.

If your child has decided he would like to participate in a hockey school or camp, sit down with him and constructively help him identify at least two areas he'd like to improve. Have him write his goals down himself for his own reference. This way, he'll have a sense of ownership over his development.

HOCKEY SCHOOLS

Many of the schools and camps geared to older players are not included here.

Atlantic

Euro Hockey Camps	Wayne, NJ
Hockey Techniques Hockey School	Various locations on
(formerly Todd Drevitch's Hockey School)	East Coast
Protechockey Camps	Lawrenceville, NJ
Skaters Edge Hockey School	Montclair, NJ

Central

Can/Am Hockey	Williams Bay, WI
	(also Welland, Ontario)
Eagle River Hockey School	Eagle River, WI
European Elite Hockey	Several locations in Illinois
The Hockey School	Spooner, WI
Next Level Hockey School	Somerset, WI
STARS Hockey Camp	Williams Bay, WI

Massachusetts

Chabot Specialized Hockey Skills School	Falmouth
Gary Dineen Hockey School	Agawam
Ice Works USA	Groton
Newton Hockey Camp	Needham
Pro Ambitions Hockey Camps	Dover
Superskills Hockey	Tewksbury

Michigan

Ferris State University Summer Hockey School	Big Rapids

Grand Rapids Hockey Camp	Grand Rapids
featuring Don Lucia	
Michigan Tech Hockey	Houghton
Development Center	
Suburban Hockey School	Farmington Hills
USA Hockey Summer School	Ann Arbor

Mid-American

Al Murdoch Hockey School	Ames, IA
Indiana/World Skating Academy	Indianapolis, IN
Kent Hockey and Goalie School	Kent, OH
NY Hockey School /Camp	Wilkes-Barre, PA
Sergei Nemchinov	
North Coast Hockey Camp	Wooster, OH
Wall Goalie School	Haverford, PA

Minnkota

Acceleration Minnesota Sports	Several locations in
Training Centers	Minnesota
Augsburg Preseason Hockey Camp	Minneapolis, MN
Bemidji Hockey School	Bemidji, MN
College of St. Benedict Summer	St. Joseph, MN
Hockey Camp	
Doug Woog Hockey Camp	Breezy Point, MN
The Goalie Club	Mankato, MN
Goaltending Dynamics	Apple Valley, MN
Development Program	
Gustavus Hockey and	St. Peter, MN
Leadership Camp	
Heartland Hockey Camp	Deerwood, MN
Hockey and Sons Camp	Faribault, MN
Hockey Town Hockey School	Warroad, MN

International Hockey Schools	Detroit Lakes, MN
International Hockey Tours	Based in MN, hockey trips to Europe
Janostin Hockey Training	Three locations in Minnesota
Line Drive Hockey	Brooklyn Park, MN
Minnesota Hockey Camps	Clark Lake, MN
Minnesota Made Hockey	Burnsville, MN
Minnesota Wild Hockey School	St. Paul, MN
NSC Hockey Development	Blaine, MN
Peak Performance Hockey Camp	Winona, MN
Rick St. Croix School of Goaltending	Two locations in Minnesota
SCSU Summer Hockey School	St. Cloud, MN
Saint Mary's University Hockey Camps	Winona, MN
Shattuck-St. Mary's Elite Hockey Schools	Faribault, MN
Stauber's Goalcrease Academy	Edina, MN
Steve Carroll Goalie School for Boys and Girls	Minneapolis, MN
Steve Guider Goalie School	Blaine, MN
United States Hockey Camp Association	Fargo, ND
Univ. of North Dakota Summer Hockey School	Grand Forks, ND
Top Dog Hockey Camps and Clinics	Three locations in Minnesota

New England

AAA Top Dog	Bridgton, ME
Camp All-Star	Kents Hill, ME

Dan McFall's Full Stride Hockey Training	South Burlington, VT
Elite Hockey Camps	Vermont and New Hampshire locations
Exeter Hockey School	Exeter, NH
RinkSport	Kingston, RI

New York

Army Hockey Camp	West Point
Boot Camp Hockey	Lake Placid
Cornell Big Red Hockey Camps	Ithaca
World Hockey Institute	Buffalo

Pacific

Camp Freeze	Paramount, CA
Great West Goalie Camp	San Diego, CA
Robby Glantz Power Skating	Sherman Oak, CA

Rocky Mountain

Bob Johnson Hockey Schools	Colorado Springs, CO
European Summer Hockey Tours	Squirts and over train in Europe
LaFontaine Hockey Schools	Bozeman, MT
Planet Hockey Ranch	Superior, CO
Rocky Mountain Hockey Schools	Evergreen, CO

Southeastern

Charlottesville Ice Park Hockey School	Charlottesville, VA
Global Hockey	Tequesta, FL
SunCoast International Hockey School	Palm Harbor, FL
The Gardens Ice House	Laurel, MD
Turcotte Stickhandling Hockey School	Based in Florida

Canada

Banff Hockey Academy	Banff, Alberta
Canlan Ice Sports Hockey Academy	Burnaby, British Columbia
PR King's Sunshine Coast Hockey School	Powell River, British Columbia
Canada Hockey Enterprises Limited	Peterborough, Ontario *(also Lake Placid, NY)*
GHA Hockey	Gloucester, Ontario
Hockey Opportunity Camp	Sundridge, Ontario
Hockey Tech International	Toronto, Ontario
Huron Hockey School	Ottawa, Ontario *(some U.S. programs)*
Jim Park Goalie School	Rexdale, Ontario
PASS Hockey Enterprises	Brampton, Ontario
Star fire International Hockey	Belleville, Ontario
Teen Ranch Hockey Camp	Calledon Village, Ontario
HMI Hockey Camp	Montreal, Quebec
Hockey Montreal International	Montreal, Quebec

Traveling or chain programs include American Hockey Schools, Christian Hockey Camps International, Gary Hebert's World Academy of Hockey, Greg Carter's European Hockey Camp, Hockey Ministries International, Laura Stamm Power Skating, Maximum Development Hockey Schools, Nike Ice Hockey Camps, Perfect Skater Hockey Schools, Planet Hockey Schools, Prime Time Hockey Summer Camps, Pro Ambitions Hockey Inc., Rick Heinz Goalie and Hockey Schools, Robby Glantz, Skating Dynamics, Skills Plus Hockey School, Sport International Hockey Academy, Turcotte Stickhandling Hockey School.

Specific information for most hockey schools and camps can be found on Internet Web sites.

YOUTH HOCKEY REFERENCES
USA Hockey

175 Bob Johnson Dr.

Colorado Springs, CO

8096-4090

719-576-8724

719-538-1160 (fax)

www.usahockey.com

Canadian Hockey Association

1600 Prom. James Naismith Dr.

Suite 607

Gloucester, Ontario

K1B 5N4

613-748-5613

613-748-5709 (fax)

www.owha.on.ca

American Sports Education Program

P.O. Box 5076

Champaign, IL

61825-5076

1-800-747-5698

6

Medic Mom

A study by Minnesota researchers found that body checking accounted for 59 percent of hockey injuries (20 percent from legal checking and 39 percent from illegal checking) and that rules violations were responsible for another 27 percent.
— Susan Gaines, "Making Hockey Safer," *Minnesota Medical Association Publications,* vol. 83, June 2000.

Hockey is a contact sport. According to MomsTeam.com, "Ice hockey is the second leading cause of winter sports injury among children." Although U.S. Mites and Squirts leagues are non-bodychecking, they'll still get hit—due to their young age and lack of ability—as they accidentally crash into each other. Yet, according to USA Hockey, most youth players will suffer injuries from contact with the boards, net posts, and the ice itself.

COMMON HOCKEY INJURIES

Bruises and sprains to the shoulders, elbows, wrists, legs, knees, and ankles become more common as the youth hockey player increases in age, according to USA Hockey's "Prevention of Hockey Injuries" section in its *Hockey Education Adult Resource (H.E.A.R.).* Since

youth hockey leagues began requiring facial masks, the once ubiqui-
tous missing teeth and scarred face dramatically decreased from the
mugs of young players. Eye injuries thankfully have become a rarity
as well in youth hockey with facial protection and strict enforcement
against high-sticking.

Today's youth hockey associations have firm guidelines requiring proper protective gear on the ice. Therefore, parents should realize that today's players are better protected from injury than players
of the past. Yet, if your child suffers an injury worse than a small
bruise, he ought to be checked out by a doctor. The rule of thumb
is simple: if you're unsure how badly he's hurt, take him to a doctor.

ICE HOCKEY INJURY PREVENTION TIPS

- Take your child for a complete physical before he begins a season of playing competitive ice hockey.
- Gear up your child in complete hockey armor, equipment that
  is HECC certified and fits perfectly.
- Have your child fitted for a mouth guard. Though he wears facial protection already, if he is hit hard he might bite his tongue
  or injure his teeth or jaw.
- Have your child stretch the muscles in his arms, legs, back,
  and neck before jumping on to the ice.
- Remind your child to play hockey with his head up.
- To avoid shoulder injury, warn your child against dropping his
  shoulder if he's about to collide into the boards or another player.
- Stress to your child that he should never skate through pain; if
  something hurts, he must get off the ice immediately and tell
  you or his coach.

- Make sure the coach has a first-aid kit. To avoid the awkwardness of appearing intrusive, simply say, "Hey, if the team hasn't got a first-aid kit together yet, I'll put one together." This is a tactful way of finding out if there is one.
- If you don't have a coach who enforces rules of play, do something about it. Talk to him. If that doesn't work, he needs to be reported to the league's board.
- Understand that, though inevitably there are risks to playing the aggressive sport of ice hockey, you can encourage your child to develop a balance between athletic aggressiveness and smart, fair play.
- Promote careful play. While aggression is good for getting the puck and shooting it in the net, reckless play rarely leads to a goal. Rather, reckless skating results in injury to other players or self-inflicted injury.
- Prevent what USA Hockey calls the "Superman Syndrome"—reckless play because players feel well protected with protective gear. Remind your player the equipment is to prevent injury from pucks, sticks, skates, boards, and ice; it is not to promote reckless skating, which USA Hockey calls "dumb hockey."

INJURY TREATMENT

You can prevent soreness and injury to your child's muscles and joints by getting him in the habit of stretching his legs and back before dressing in his gear and once again before entering the ice. Possible ice hockey injuries are listed below with tips to alleviate your child's pain and discomfort:

Blisters—Break the blister with a sterilized needle, apply an antibiotic ointment to it, and cover it with a Band-Aid. Put a dab of

Vaseline inside the skate on the area where the blister occurred to decrease the amount of friction between the skate and the affected area of the foot.

Bruises—RICE (rest, ice, compression, elevation).

Sprains—If you suspect a sprain, administer RICE and take your child to a doctor.

Breaks—A rare occurrence in youth ice hockey, but if you suspect a break, go to the nearest emergency room. Your child will be off the ice for at least two months.

Knee Pain—In most instances, RICE will help. If you suspect out-of-the-ordinary knee discomfort, schedule an appointment with a doctor who is familiar with sports injuries.

Concussions—Even with a properly fitting helmet, it is possible for your child to fall hard enough to suffer a concussion. If he took an unusually hard hit in the head, do not hesitate having him checked out by a doctor as soon as possible. He should not return to the ice until all signs of headache and fatigue have disappeared.

Instructor Troy Barron teaches Mini-Mites at St. Clair Shores Civic Arena in Michigan how to pass the puck heads up.

HEADS-UP HOCKEY

If you pay close attention to a youth hockey practice, you'll note a recurring instruction from the coaches. "Heads up," a coach will call across the ice—over and over again. The direction is not only to enforce better stickhandling. It is for the player's safety. Reinforce this instruction to your child. Heads-up hockey protects the neck and spine in two ways: the first is obvious—the player sees where he's going; the second is that heads-up play forces the natural curve of the neck, which makes the neck more flexible upon impact. If the head is down, the neck is tensed, and, upon impact, the chances for injury dramatically increase. When a player runs into another player or the boards, his head stops suddenly while his body continues to move, putting great strain on his neck and spine. A fracture or break of one or more vertebrae could result. Certainly, spinal discs and muscles will be strained. In the heads-down position the neck is tensed and rigid. Even skating at a slow speed and colliding could cause great damage if the head is down. The heads-up skater, however, has maximum flexibility in his neck and spine and is able to take a hit with far less chance of suffering a spinal injury.

USA Hockey's coaching clinic materials cite the "Heads up!" command as "the single most important thing to know and do to

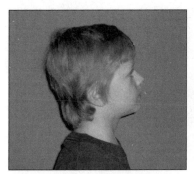

With the head up, a skater has maximum neck and spine flexibility.

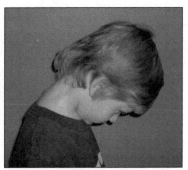

With the head down, a skater's neck is tensed and rigid and more vulnerable to injury.

prevent head injuries." Be sure, Mom, to remind your player to skate heads up. Chances are that his coach will be drilling this into his hockey psyche as well. If the coach is not frequently yelling out "Heads up," especially to novice players, he ought to be.

A young player also ought to remember never to duck. If he sees a check coming at him, he has to skate through it with his head up. (Although bodychecking is illegal in Mites and Squirts levels, it happens.) Remembering not to duck will keep the player's head out of the check. The impact will be less severe if he doesn't stop or slow down and stays in motion while skating through a check. Your player's coach should have taught him to do the following in order to avoid checking injury:

- Skate parallel to the boards.
- Move out quickly.
- Keep the feet in motion.
- Use arms and legs to absorb the shock of the body check.
- Skate with feet apart, legs bent, and with a low center of gravity.
- Avoid contact with the boards as much as possible; never have the head down near the boards.

DEALING WITH SPINAL INJURY

If you suspect a player has suffered a spinal injury, make sure someone gets help immediately. The coach will probably be the first one to attend to him on the ice. Stay near the bench, and allow the coach to stay with him to keep him calm until the paramedics arrive. Your child's USA Hockey-certified coach has been taught to look for these symptoms after spinal impact:

- Pain at the cite of contact
- Tingling in arms or legs

- Loss of movement
- Sharp pain in arms or legs

While awaiting paramedics, the coach will ensure that the child's airway is clear. He will monitor the ABCs—airway, breathing, and circulation—as he is working to keep the player calm and still. He will put a blanket or jacket over the player to keep him warm. No one except the paramedics should move the player off the ice.

Bell Ringers

Concussions have some goofy monikers in hockey. You might hear them referred to as "bell ringers" or "brain dimmers." Slapstick comedy and cartoons portray hits on the head in a funny way, and even in real life a kid with a strong hit to the head might make a silly remark or look goofy. Nevertheless, a hit to the head must be dealt with in a serious manner. In fact, if a player is not acting like himself, if his reaction is indeed goofy, this is a telltale sign that he needs immediate medical attention. Concussions are serious and require serious medical care. Kim Tinkham, in an article in *USA Hockey Magazine*, described what happens to the brain with a concussion this way: "In layman's terms it would be similar to pressing the reset button on a computer and waiting for it to reboot. You are taking the chance that what you haven't saved on your hard drive will not be there the next time you go to look for it."

Even if an impact to the head seems minor, coaches and parents must react quickly and smartly. Your first step, Mom, must be your mom's-gut diagnosis—ruling a concussion in or out. If you're unsure, then the best practice is to play it safe and protect your player by taking him to the emergency room. The maxim is, "When in doubt, sit them out." A doctor will treat the case individually based on your child's medical history and behavior after the hit.

DETERMINING IF IT MIGHT BE A CONCUSSION

If your child has these symptoms following a hit to the head, take him to be evaluated by a medical doctor:

- Seems unaware of his surroundings
- Exhibits memory loss
- Loses consciousness for any length of time
- Loses balance
- Complains of seeing flashing lights or of hearing ringing in the ears
- Has blurred vision
- Has slurred speech
- Has strangely dilated pupils or pupils that are unevenly dilated
- Suddenly feels sleepy
- Displays signs of altered personality
- Is slow to respond to simple questions
- Suffers from nausea

According to the First International Conference on Concussion in Sport, if a player exhibits symptoms of a concussion, he should:

- Not be allowed to return to the game or practice
- Not be left unmonitored by an adult
- Be taken to a doctor as soon as possible
- Only return to skating upon his doctor's recommendation

If a player is conscious, but seems disoriented, remove him from play and check on him every few minutes. Ask him to respond to some questions so that you can monitor whether or not he is developing amnesia or any other symptoms of concussion. Ask him where he is and what the names of his teammates are. Ask him about the injury, where it is specifically and how it happened. Check his stored memory by asking him the name of the last team his team played. Ask for details about the game. Ask the player to recite three words, then ask him to recite the same three words about five minutes later. If the player has suffered a Grade-3 concussion, meaning he has lost consciousness, the player must receive medical attention from paramedics as soon as possible and be transported from the rink by ambulance.

If your player has suffered any kind of head injury, USA Hockey rules mandate that the coach cannot return him to play during the game of the injury. If he requires medical attention, your coach will require a doctor's note to return him to the ice.

The best thing you can do to prevent your child from suffering a concussion is to buy him an HECC-certified helmet that fits perfectly and a made-to-fit mouth guard, which can be fitted by a local dentist. Though your child might complain about the fit of the helmet until he gets used to it, be sure that it fits snugly. If your child can move his head inside the helmet, it is too big. Wearing a loose-fitting helmet sets a player up for head injury, especially if he suffers a hit to the side of the head. Always fasten the straps snugly, but not tightly. His chin should fit well in the chin cup. If you purchase a used helmet, keep in mind that HECC certification is good for only five years. Though hockey helmets are expandable, a child's growing noggin should not be in the same helmet for more than two years. If a helmet gets cracked, thank God the crack was not in your child's head—then throw the helmet away. Your skater needs a new one now. If the face cage is bent, pitch that too, as well as a plastic shield that is cracked or scratched.

HOCKEY FIRST-AID KIT

Be sure that your team's coach has a first-aid kit. You might volunteer to gather the contents, which should include:

- A list of emergency contact information for team members
- A box of Band-Aids
- Two rolls of plastic tape
- Several sterile gauze pads
- Several ziplock bags (for assembling ice packs)
- A chemical ice pack
- Two pairs of latex gloves
- Disinfectant wipes
- Scissors
- Triple antibiotic ointment
- Tooth-saver kit
- Saline solution and contact case
- Inhalers for asthmatic players (supplied by parent of asthmatic)

You also may want to include a mouth-to-mouth breathing device for a player requiring CPR and an oral airway to attend to a player having a seizure.

Always make sure the players stay hydrated. A parent should be assigned the job of supplying water bottles for practices and games.

PREVENTION—WARM-UPS AND STRETCHING

USA Hockey recommends the following exercises for injury prevention:

Jumping Jacks, seven minutes total

legs only	1 min., 30 secs.
arms only	30 secs.
full	1 min., 30 secs.

cross	1 min., 30 secs.
cross arms	30 secs.
combo cross	1 min., 30 secs.

Stretch problem areas
Neck stretches
    tilting head side-to-side for slow six count
    turning head to one side and the other for slow six count
Skipping opposite arms/opposite legs
Power skipping
Side slides—low
Grapevines
Leg swings—diagonal, forward, and back
Jumps—forward to back, side to side, and rotation

7

Team Manager Mom

The thing that I'll take [with me] will not necessarily be the championships. It'll be the people—the good athletes and their good attitudes. Those will be my fondest memories.
—Herb Brooks, coach of the miraculous 1980 Team USA

The role of a house team manager is frequently filled by a hockey mom. Often she is married to the coach and, as fate and its lack of volunteers would have it, has inherited the role as a result. If your husband is a coach, you may suddenly find yourself in the daunting role of team manager. Get ready, Mom, a team manager wears many hats and has an extremely important, behind-the-scenes job to do. (But moms are used to wearing many hats, right?)

While the coach sets the tone for the team, the team manager sets the tone for the parents. The coach works the bench, while the team manager works the bleachers. Players and parents will come into the season with high hopes and expectations for a year of fun and hockey development. Looking forward to nail-biting competition and fair play across the league, players and parents require their team's leaders—head coach, assistant coaches, and team manger—to be dedicated, enthusiastic, and well organized. It's a lot to ask of people who are not being paid for all the energy, emotion, and time that's required of them. Mom, if later your mother's legacy includes tributes to you by your child and her teammates as "that way-cool hockey mom who managed our team way back when," that's payment enough, right? If you're recognized by all or most of your fellow team parents (chances are you won't please everyone) as a fantastic team manager, then mission accomplished. Team management is a kudos-worthy task, certainly something to add to your résumé. The clincher is that probably you'll hardly be thanked for all you do as a season's management is unfolding.

To get off on the right foot, be organized early on (preseason), communicate the head coach's and your expectations, advertise the team's volunteer needs, and provide dates and details for anticipated major fund-raisers and tournaments as soon as possible. Be approachable for players and parents, smile a lot, and, as always, practice heads-up hockey parenting while facing the ups and downs of managing a youth hockey team.

THE DRAFT AND REGISTRATION

Around draft time, which is in August, your USA-Hockey certified coach and you will attend pre-draft meetings organized by your league's board. You will probably attend the draft with the coaches and begin working on roster paperwork. Soon there will be a division practice-scheduling meeting that you must attend and participate in. About that time you will be busy notifying players' parents that their child has been drafted by your team. You'll introduce yourself and notify them of the first team meeting (perhaps a player and parent preseason hockey party). At the first meeting you will collect the documentation that your league's registrar requires for your team's registration portfolio or packet. By mid-September, your division will have created a game schedule. You may be required to attend that scheduling meeting.

THE TEAM PORTFOLIO

- Team application form
- Player roster form
- Copy of birth certificate for each rostered player
- USA Hockey individual membership registration form for each rostered player, head coach, assistant coaches, and manager
- Waiver and release for each registered participant
- Consent to treat form for each rostered player
- Sanctioned game score sheets

TEAM-MONEY MANAGEMENT

As team manager you will be in charge of buying ice time. You should designate a parent as treasurer, whose duties will include opening a team checking account; making deposits; tracking income and expenditures with written statements for you and the division representative; and writing checks for the team ice, equipment, clothing, tournament fees, and so on.

Begin the quest of recruiting sponsorship from area businesses to defray the cost of jerseys, for example. Start with your team parents, who may own businesses themselves. Others will know friends or have relatives whose business might be interested in sponsoring a youth hockey team.

During the season, you and the coach may decide that you'd like to sell a session of ice or buy more ice time. You can log on to "Ice on Sale" at www.iceonsale.com for this purpose, or you can do it the old-fashioned way—display a "need ice" or "ice for sale" flyer at your rink.

BILLING FOR ICE

The following is the formula you'll use to figure out the monthly ice bill for each player:

Cost of ice per hour (about $250)
 x ice hours per month (12 to 15)
+ team costs, including tournament fees and ice equipment, like cones and pucks
- fund-raising revenue
÷ number of players on your team
= each player's ice bill

Your team must pay its ice bill in advance, starting in early September to kick off the regular hockey season. From then on, collect ice payments during the last week of each month for the following month's payment to the rink.

DELEGATING

Critical to managing a hockey team is managing the hockey parents. Good team managers set the momentum for a good attitude among the team parents. A practical way to do this is to put the parents to work. Delegate several of your team management responsibilities to them. This creates the opportunity for the parents to work as a team and develop an atmosphere of camaraderie just like the bond their children are developing on the ice. Stay on top of it; yet do not micromanage. You'll lose your volunteers if you take back control over the responsibilities you have just delegated. Designate one parent to jersey-care duty, another to water bottle duty. Choose a volunteer to act as team treasurer, another as team publications manager. Assign a few volunteers to a team fund-raising committee that includes a "jug mom," someone who collects money among spectators when your team scores. You need to leave yourself free for managing and budgeting ice time and tournaments, a responsibility that must be handled with great care to detail. You cannot let yourself become bogged down with every task. Just as you run your household with attention to detail, patience, organization, and delegation, you must run the affairs of the team efficiently and wisely.

A great way my oldest son's team manager delegated duties was by throwing a preseason hockey team party. She organized it immediately after the draft. At the party, she gathered everyone to describe responsibilities she needed volunteers for. Then she left the parents with sign-up sheets. She had all the volunteers she needed before the first practice. Working together so early helped the parents to get to know one another, too. The team atmosphere remained friendly during the entire season. I believe our active, early-on commitment to helping the team made us quickly comfortable with one another.

Hockey mom Linda DeHooghe, with son Edin, buying pizza kits to support St. Clair Shores Hockey Association parents' club fund-raiser. Pictured also are Sue Pode, 2005–06 club president, and Luanne Romano, 2004–05 club president.

The St. Clair Shores Hockey Association Parents' Club commences a monthly meeting. A house team manager must be sure that there is at least one team parent representing the team on the club, which overseas several undertakings to support players.

The Team Manager is Responsible for:

- Registering players
- Assembling the team portfolio
- Supplying the team first-aid kit
- Ensuring that water bottles are available and working
- Making sure the team has pucks and cones
- Ordering home and visitor jerseys and socks
- Ordering travel gear, such as team-logo sweaters or jackets and hats for players, coaches, and the manager
- Scheduling games and practices
- Paying for ice time
- Registering the team in tournaments, and communicating with tournament organizers

- Delivering copies of schedules to the players' parents
- Maintaining the team Web site and team publications
- Handling the team finances
- Communicating encouragement to players and parents

COMMUNICATION

Just as the coach lets players know up front what he expects in behavior, state to parents how they're expected to behave in order to maintain a healthy team spirit and experience in the stands and in the lobby. Work with your coach to develop and communicate to parents and players your team's code of ethics and discipline policy. Stress to parents that their social and emotional involvement in the team must be positive input and that as team manager you will work with coaches and league representatives to confront any negative behavior you see in the stands, locker room, or lobby. Inform parents that unruly parents will be required to leave the arena. Clearly state up front that reasonable constructive feedback in the spirit of cooperation is welcome, but warn that you will not be bullied by emotion-driven criticism.

You or a parent who has volunteered will prepare several handouts throughout the season, including:

- Monthly practice and game schedules
- Team roster with parents' names and contact information
- Tournament information
- Fund-raising event and benchmark information
- Ice payment dates
- Team stats and standings information
- Hockey parenting tips and encouragement
- League and division news

USA Hockey offers all youth hockey teams and leagues free Web hosting through USAHockey.com. You can easily post your handouts here electronically, but always distribute paper handouts as well. Before posting pictures of your players on the Web, be sure you have permission from parents.

An exceptional team manager will also stay on top of who's ill, injured, or mourning a recent death among team families. She will organize mailing cards or sending flowers on behalf of the team.

FUND-RAISING POSSIBILITIES

- Bowling event with raffle
- Dinner-dance with silent auction
- Raffle of prizes donated by parents
- Bottle drive (if your state has a returnable bottle and can law)
- Newspaper drive
- Restaurant work—some restaurants will let team parents come in and wait on tables; then they'll donate a percentage of receipts to the team. Plus the team keeps its tips.
- Jug mom—a hockey mom volunteer who collects change from spectators each time the team scores a goal
- Spaghetti dinner or pancake breakfast

TOURNAMENTS

You will be responsible for the logistics of getting your team signed up for tournaments, paying for the tournaments, and following up with tournament registrar personnel. When researching tournaments, find out about each tournament's specific rules. With the head coach, narrow down a list of a few tournament options for your team. At that first preseason meeting with team players and parents, mention the host cities and dates of these tournaments in which you're considering entering the team. This will give parents a chance to voice their concerns about traveling distance or dates and help you make a decision about which tournaments to enter.

Register for tournaments early in the season. Follow up with frequent phone calls until you have confirmation that your team is invited. Then immediately reserve the team's overnight accommodations. The best hockey-team-friendly hotels become booked quickly.

Tournaments are vacation-like in a lot of ways. Not only do players and hockey parents attend, but so do players' siblings. Make sure your team stays at a hotel that includes facilities for fun during the team's free time, such as a swimming pool. Research and communicate to team families the area's kid-friendly restaurants and attractions. You might want to organize one event for all the families to attend, such as a dinner at a pizza parlor. Be sure not to overschedule

A popular hockey-team destination, Hockey Heroes Museum Kitchen Bar, in Traverse City, Michigan, is a mini museum of hockey memorabilia. Here a player checks out the restaurant's penalty box.

your team; allow families family time and players kid time. Ask parents who have teenagers who will be traveling with the group if you can organize an evening out for the parents with their teens assigned to paid babysitting duty.

THINKING OF COACHING?

As in many youth sports, most youth hockey coaches work on a volunteer basis. A coach ought to coach because he enjoys the game and enjoys working with kids. If you meet these qualifications, you can take the next step by getting certified. If you'll be coaching in the United States, USA Hockey offers coaching clinics, a track program for volunteers (as well as a professional program). Certificates are earned according to the level, which is set by age category and house or competitive category. If you cannot enroll in a certification program, you could study a book published by the American Sport Education Program, called Coaching Youth Hockey, which is one title in its Coaching Youth Series. Most youth hockey associations in the United States require USA Hockey certification. Though the associations are governed by state or regional bodies and their rules, USA Hockey is the national, unifying organization that sets the guidelines for these bodies.

If you'll be coaching in Canada, the Canadian Hockey Association offers coaching clinics as part of its National Coaching Certificate Program (NCCP). The program consists of four certification levels, based on the experience and competitiveness level of the teams to be coached.

8

Encourager Mom

It [hockey parenting] began and it continued with "being there." Being there to be the ones who were the nurturers, the disciplinarians, the encouragers, the teachers, the trainers, the role models, the coaches, the photographers, the fans.

—Jay Blysma, in *So Your Son Wants to Play in the NHL*
by Dan and Jay Blysma

The experts have told me that not all hockey players have hockey sense. I say not all hockey moms have hockey-mom sense. Like a skater who hogs the puck, a mom lacking hockey-mom sense has tunnel vision. Her motivation at the rink is to see that her son and herself are glorified. Though she may seemingly strut through the rink heads up, her blinders of pride and selfishness have blocked any awareness of the players and parents around her and play vision for the team. A mom lacking hockey-mom sense is not an encourager, even to her own child. She sucks the fun out of youth hockey.

HEADS-UP HOCKEY-MOM ENCOURAGEMENT

Let your heads-up hockey-mom strategy evolve from your sense of parenting. As Jay Blysma states in the excerpt above, the first step in being an encourager in youth hockey is being there to fill all the roles the job of hockey parent entails. While a mom with no hockey-mom sense is there physically, she is shortchanging her child by not filling all those roles. She might be trainer but not nurturer, photographer but not role model, teacher but not encourager. You might find that as you nurture and encourage your own child, you're moved to say a few kind words to the child whose mom, unfortunately, lacks hockey-mom sense. As you tap into your sense of hockey-mom parenting to practice good heads-up hockey parenting, you will undeniably become a role model to all the children— and their parents.

The St. Clair Shores, Michigan, Mite Panthers are treated to slushies after a game, which is a tradition. From left are Zach Vogel, Marshall Moise, Nick Cusmano, Shane Doig, Tyler Creagh, and Jacob Troyer.

BULLIES

You can use the bad behavior of bullying players and bullying parents as a launching pad for discussing with your child positive behavior and the consequences of bad behavior. Discuss what motivates someone to act like a bully. Is a bully afraid of something? Angry? Hurt? Ignorant? Tell your child that just as there are bullying children, there are bullying parents. Quote the words of the NHL's winningest coach, Scotty Bowman, who said, "Every boo on the road is a cheer."

Without being catty, talk to your player about ugly incidents among hockey parents, which you know he has witnessed rather close up. Explain why and how these adults acted wrongly. Perhaps you made a mistake in judgment at the rink and blew off at a linesman or another parent. Tell your child how sorry you are and what you'll do to resolve what happened.

JUST A BOY

He stands at the blue line with his heart pumping fast
The score is tied, the die has been cast
Mom and Dad cannot help him; he stands all alone
A goal at this moment could send the team home
The puck nears the goal; he shoots and he misses
There's a groan from the crowd, with some boos and some hisses
A thoughtless voice cries, "Throw out the bum"
Tears fill his eyes, the game's no longer fun
Remember, he's just a boy who stands all alone
So open your heart and give him a break
For it's at moments like this a man you can make
Keep this in mind when you hear someone forget
He's just a boy and not a man yet

—Author Unknown

Mite Shane Doig listens to his coach's directions.

LOSING

It's more fun to win a game, naturally. Nonetheless, lost games are just as important as won games to a player's development. If your child is disappointed after a lost game, explain this point to her. Developing your game is what matters. It takes time, which in hockey translates to lots of ice time in practices and in games, both winning and losing. If she feels particularly badly about a certain mistake she made during game play, explain that the whole team owns the loss, just as it owns its wins. Remind her that losing and making mistakes are part of mastering the sport. Tell her what Edmonton Oilers general manager Glen Sather said, "There is no escalator to success—only steps."

If its a goalie you're consoling, my hat goes off to you. I have great admiration for goalie moms. I can't imagine how difficult it must be to see a puck get past your child and then hear the opposing side roar with cheers at the same moment. A goalie mom once told me that in comforting and encouraging her Mite goalie, she says, "Hey, the other team had to get by five other guys to get the puck near you. You're the last line of defense, and you cannot successfully defend your net every single time." Then they discuss all the saves he made. If you parent a goalie, be sure to note and acknowledge all of his saves. If you parent a position player, take the time to encourage your team's goalie and his mom.

JERSEY QUILTS

You could accumulate dozens of jerseys during your youth hockey journey, especially if your child tends to participate frequently in hockey schools and camps. Some moms have cleverly turned their child's jersey collection into a quilt. Melissa's T-Shirts, Quilts, and Crafts in Flint, Michigan, will put a quilt together for you

for a reasonable fee. Contact owner Melissa Hintz. She provides information on her Web site: www.melsquilts.com. Above is one of Melissa's quilts, a twin-bed-sized quilt made from ten hockey jerseys.

HEADS-UP HOCKEY MOM DOS AND DON'TS
Do

- Teach your child with positive suggestions, not criticism. Sometimes your child might be upset with his performance and want your help. In such a situation, offer advice in a fun way. For example, instead of saying, "You're not skating to the puck fast enough," offer a fun tip like this: "Pretend that puck is your favorite toy and it's about to get lost. Go and get it like that." In the locker room before a game, I sometimes whisper to my boys, "You're a lion. The puck is your pride's dinner. Go get it."

Don't

- Criticize your child's performance—ever—in front of teammates or privately.

Do

- Celebrate the effort in every game by all of the players.

Don't

- Criticize any of the players in front of your child. Chances are that your child likes her teammates and even the other players in the division; don't go and ruin that for her.

Do

- Discuss with your child's coach ways to support your child's hockey development. If your child has indicated to you a desire to improve his game, ask the coach about ways you can help your child develop, such as off-ice activities to help him improve stick-handling or speed.

Don't

- Complain about the coach to your child. Putting a child in the quandary of whether to heed the hockey advice of mom or the coach is unfair and no fun for the child.

Do

- Stress the importance of the friendships you and your child are making at the rink. Remind your child that youth hockey is about building character and lasting memories, as much as it is about developing skills.

Don't

- Associate your child's points accumulation with being a good person. So much of a child's self-worth depends on how she believes you, her mother, perceives her. She ought to feel that you care more about her character than her athletic talent and performance.

Do

- Discuss with your child the consequences of positive and negative hockey behavior. Use incidents at the rink as a launching pad for discussion. Also, reassure your child that if participants in his division are not abiding by the official rules of fair play, they will pay the consequences. Meanwhile, insist to your child that he should only concern himself with playing his game well, never mind what others are doing wrong.

Don't

- Encourage your child to tattle on teammates or retaliate against opponents.

Do

- Teach your player about will—the heartfelt belief that you can win can trump your opponent's skills. Tell her the story of the 1980 Team USA win over the Soviet Union.

Don't

- Talk about how great an opposing team is in front of your child as if to imply that her team will surely lose.

Do

- Encourage your child to find his game. Tell him that as a writer finds his voice, or a painter finds his technique, a hockey player finds, owns, and hones his game.

Don't

- Force a particular style of playing the game on your child, especially if you have never played yourself. To own his youth hockey experience, he must develop his game in his own time in his own way.

Recognize and carefully communicate to your child that part of developing a good hockey player attitude is the knowledge that there are better players out there. Striving to become as good, or better, is a positive thing.

Because the game is about people, not numbers, tap into your hockey-mom sense to hone your awareness of those around you who are open for receiving a pass of encouragement. Then encourage enthusiastically and selflessly, tape-to-tape.

Hockey mom Anne Bloomfield with her son Alex, a Mite with St. Clair Shores
Hockey Association in Michigan.   *Photo by George Bloomfield*

Glossary

alley-oop pass—a set-up pass to a teammate, often the center, who's driving toward the net; from the French *allez*, meaning "go" in the imperative

assist—a pass to a player that immediately leads to a goal scored; game and season records are kept on an individual's number of assists

attacking zone—the offensive zone, the area between the blue line and the goal line

back-check—covering an opponent while skating back to one's own goal

bag skate—skating sprint laps; a coach might call for a bag skate as a means of getting out-of-shape skaters into shape or evaluating player endurance

barn—a hockey arena

biscuit—the puck

blueliner—a defenseman

blue lines—blue lines across the ice that are sixty feet from goal

boards—the wall around the rink

bodycheck—covering an opponent by hitting him with one's body

breakaway—a one-man rush toward the offensive goal, also referred to as one-on-zero, a fast break, an all-alone, an offensive break, head start, and break in on goal

breakout—movement of a team in possession of the puck out of its defensive zone

breakout pass—a pass to a breaking teammate

bulging the twine—scoring a goal

catlike reflexes—play swiftness, usually referring to the goalie's ability to block the puck with his body or catch the puck in his glove

center—the middle player on an offensive line

center ice—the neutral area between the two blue lines

center line—the red stripe across the ice, midway between the two goals

changing on the fly—substituting players without stopping play

checking—covering an opponent to prevent him from gaining good position on the ice

cherry-picking—an offensive player waiting behind play for a break-out pass

chiclets—teeth (wearing a mask and mouth guard will prevent your child from "spitting chiclets")

chirping—a player talking to an opposing player or whining and complaining about a call a referee made against him

clearing the puck—shooting the puck either away from the front of the net or out of the defensive zone into neutral territory

crease—a four-foot-by-eight-foot area in front of the goal, which is out of bounds for attacking players not in possession of the puck

cycling—maintaining puck possession between the forwards as they are in constant motion, essential to a triangle offense

dangle—(a verb) has to do with savvy stickhandling and puck control

defensemen—the two players who cover the front of their goal, working to prevent opponents from gaining good position in that area and from shooting the puck past them into goal

deke—a fake move of the head, shoulders, stick, et cetera, to confuse the opponent and move him out of position *delayed penalty*—a team cannot be more than two players short on the ice; so if a team is down two and commits a penalty, serving the penalty will commence when one of the current penalties has terminated

delayed whistle—if a breach is committed against the team in possession of the puck, the referee will not blow the whistle to stop play until the offending team touches the puck

diver—a player who fakes falling in order to confuse referees and to get them to call a tripping, hooking, or interference penalty on an opposing player who was in the vicinity of the dive

face-off—the referee dropping the puck between two opposing players to start a game or resume a game after a violation, time-out, or period break

finisher—a frequent goal scorer

forechecking—covering an opponent in his own end

forwards—the two players on either side of the center in an offensive line

freezing the puck—the goalie catching the puck or falling on top of it to stop play

goal—the completion of getting the puck across the goal line to register a scoring goal

goal judge—an off-ice official who sits behind the goal and outside the boards to determine if the puck enters the goal

goal line—the red stripe between the goalposts that extend to the side boards

hat trick—three goals scored by a single player in a single game

headman—(a verb) moving the puck up by passing it to a teammate

hip check—a legal check in checking leagues, by which a player bumps an opponent with the side of his body or hip

hockey sense—keen intuition, awareness, and foresight in game situations that lead to savvy playmaking, scoring, and defense of the net *icing*—when both teams have equal number of players on the ice, the puck cannot be shot from behind the center red line to the opponent's goal line without being touched

goon—a large player who often blocks opponents; in the NHL these are the "enforcers," the guys who are good at annoying opponents

grinder—a thoroughly aggressive player, who gives 100 percent for his team

line—the line of offense, or attacking line, made up of the forwards and center

loafer—a player who is not hustling enough

lumber—a hockey stick

minor officials—the officials off the ice, including the goal judges, timers, and scorers

neutral zone—the center area between the two blue lines

offside—moving ahead of the puck in the attacking (offensive) zone

one-timer shot—when a player simultaneously receives the puck and shoots it on net in one swift motion

Pinocchio effect—the difficulty of training the hands to work in a rhythm different from the feet

playmaker—the distinction a player earns for making three assists in one game

point—the area near the blue line in the offensive zone where the offensive team's defensemen position themselves. Passing between defensemen is "point to point passing," while a forward playing back in defense is "playing the point"

poke check—covering an opponent by jabbing the stick at the puck in order to force the opponent to lose possession of it

power play—play time when a team has a one- or two-player advantage because of penalties committed by the opposing team

puck hog—a loan maverick player who doesn't pass the puck to teammates, who seeks to bring the puck to goal himself so that he can bring attention and glory to himself instead of to the team

puck shy—description of a player who flinches from a puck coming in his direction

referee's crease—the area in front of the timer's table, which is restricted from players while the referee is reporting a penalty

roofing—shooting the puck on net by lifting it at a sharp angle, to under the top of the net

saucer pass—passing the puck off the blade of the stick to give it a spin, like a Frisbee tossed spinning, straight and parallel to the ground

screen—the positioning of the forwards to block the opposing goalie's view of the puck

shift—the period of time a forward line or defensive pair are out on the ice

shot blocker—a player who not only blocks with his stick but also with his body

slap shot—a shot of the puck preceded by a wide, sweeping backswing by the shooter

slot—the unmarked area in front of the net, about ten to fifteen feet in diameter

slew-foot—an illegal, dangerous maneuver by which a player puts his skate behind an opposing player's foot to force him to fall backward

spinorama—a 180-degree spin by the player in possession of the puck

sweep check—covering an opponent by going down on one knee and sweeping the stick along the ice to steal the puck away from the opponent

tape-to-tape—the flawless pass (stick-to-stick)

the room—the fraternity and solidarity of the team, the sanctum of the team where what's said stays within the team ("stays in the room")

tic-tac-toe—three rapid, flawless passes

top end—the best players on a team

traffic—putting a "screen" in front of the opposing goalie

trap—a defensive tactic involving the designation of one to two defensemen and/or one to two forwards, depending on the situation, to stay back

twig—a hockey stick

wing—(left wing, right wing) a forward skating on one side of the center player

wraparound—from behind the opposing goal, wrapping the puck around the goalpost and into the goal

wrist shot—a short, quick, effective shot made by snapping the puck directly against the blade of the stick

Zamboni—the machine that resurfaces the ice between periods

zebra—a term for a referee

Bibliography and Further Reading

BOOKS

Andreen, Jan, and Barbara Sommons. *A Zamboni Is Not a Dessert.* Philadelphia: Xlibris, 2001.

Blysma, Dan, and Jay Blysma. *So Your Son Wants to Play in the NHL.* Chelsea, MI: Sleeping Bear Press, 1998.

Davidson, John, and John Steinbreder. *Hockey for Dummies.* 2nd ed. New York: Hungry Minds, 2000.

Frayne, Trent. *Famous Hockey Players.* New York: Dodd, Mead & Company, 1973.

Harari, P. J., and Dave Ominsky. *Ice Hockey Made Simple: A Spectator's Guide.* 4th ed. Manhattan Beach, CA: First Base Sports, 2002.

Hollander, Zander. *The Hockey News Hockey Almanac.* Detroit: Visible Ink Press, 1999.

Howe, Gordie, and Colleen Howe. *And Howe!* Traverse City, MI: Power Play Publications, 1995.

McDonell, Chris, ed. *The Game I'll Never Forget: 100 Hockey Stars' Stories*. Buffalo, NY: Firefly Books, 2002.

———. *Hockey's Greatest Stars*. Buffalo, NY: Firefly Books, 2004.

———, ed. *Shooting from the Lip: Hockey's Best Quotes and Quips*. Buffalo, NY: Firefly Books, 2004.

Murphy, Shane. *The Cheers and the Tears: A Healthy Alternative to the Dark Side of Youth Sports Today*. San Francisco: Jossey-Bass, 1999.

Urstadt, Bryant, ed. *The Greatest Hockey Stories Ever Told*. Guilford, CT: Lyons Press, 2004.

Wolff, Rick. *Good Sports: The Concerned Parent's Guide to Competitive Youth Sports*. Champaign. IL: Sagamore Publishing, 1998.

OTHER

www.ESPN.com

Hockey Education Adult Resource (H.E.A.R.), instructional publication by USA Hockey, Colorado Springs, CO

www.MomsTeam.com

www.NHL.com

USA Hockey Magazine (official publication of USA Hockey and USA Hockey In-line), Colorado Springs, CO

Index